ROGER A. FA

WHERE DREAMS COME TRUE

A HISTORY OF MAPLEBROOK SCHOOL

outskirts
press

Outskirts Press, Inc.
http://www.outskirtspress.com

ISBN: 978-1-4327-7892-7

Outskirts Press and the "OP" logo are trademarks belonging to Outskirts Press, Inc.

PRINTED IN THE UNITED STATES OF AMERICA

PREFACE

When I first arrived on the campus of Maplebrook School in September of 1979 I was struck by its beauty and warmth. I was to meet Mr. Lon Adams the Headmaster to interview for a position as a part time School Psychologist. Mr. Adams had scheduled two students to give me a tour of the school. Tara and Ted showed me the academic building, dining hall, dorms and gym and told me how very much they enjoyed being students at Maplebrook.

In the thirty-eight years since that first tour of the school I have learned that Maplebrook is a very special place and decided to write a history of the school so that its uniqueness and warmth could be better understood by future generations.

I reviewed minutes of Board meetings since 1951, the year the first board of trustees convened. I reviewed yearbooks dating back to 1966 and other school documents. Also information I gleaned from conversations with alumni and parents during my tenure at Maplebrook. I conducted interviews with staff, students and parents.

Internet sites like newspapers.com and ancestry.com yielded additional helpful information that helped give a better picture of the early years.

TABLE OF CONTENTS

INTRODUCTION

Most of us assume we have always had public schools in the United States, that they were part of the Constitution and therefore are an essential part of our democratic system.

According to Sam Blumenthal, who wrote *Is Public Education Necessary*, in 1981, "The US Constitution does not mention education anywhere. It was left up to the states, parents, religious denominations and school proprietors to deal with. True, in the early days of New England, towns were required to maintain a common school supported and controlled by the local citizenship. This had been done to make sure that children learned to read so that they could read the Bible and go on to higher education." Blumenthal goes on to say, "There was much homeschooling, private tutoring, private academics, church schools and dames schools for very young children. There was no compulsory school attendance and no centralized State control over curriculum."

Private schools in America historically date back to the Catholic missionary schools opened in Florida and Louisiana in the sixteenth century. The distinction between public and private was not an issue in colonial North America. Schools were frequently founded because of the combined efforts of religious and civil authorities. No one pattern existed across the colonies. Some schools were free, some were supported by a variety of financial sources, and some relied solely on tuition. In New England, there were town schools which existed alongside private schools. By the end of the colonial period, the institution of school was firmly established on the American continent. But nothing existed like the modern concept of public education – free, compulsory, universal schooling.

Men such as Benjamin Franklin, Thomas Jefferson, George Washington and Noah Webster were among those who saw the importance of intelligent leadership. They believed in an informed citizen base and an educated professional class. Their proposals had minimal impact on the structure of schools in the colonies. Semi-public village/town schools existed side by side with private schools and charity schools for the poor. During the nineteenth century, schooling was available to most without a government mandate. Diversity of schooling co-existed with both private and public schools.

When George Washington ended his two terms as first President of the United States, he left with some advice to the fledgling nation. In his farewell address of 1796, Washington suggested a public education system. He saw the importance of well-educated citizens who possessed an enlightened public opinion. Although Washington never lived to see the establishment of such a system, his words influenced future leaders. Jefferson, among others, argued for informed and educated citizens that would result in a happier and freer American public; however, resistance to centralized government control of education was strong. Americans favored private education ventures and local control.

The nineteenth century is often referred to as the "Common School Period" because American education transitioned from a mostly private system to an increased number of public schools.

Students able to attend early nineteenth century schools were oftentimes mixed in with adults in overcrowded classrooms with few textbooks and materials. After the war of 1812, the American Public began to take greater notice of the poor education practices that existed in their educational system. During the 1820s and 1830s many urban centers doubled and tripled their populations due to immigration. This increased the desire for more public schools. Noted educator Calvin Stone warned, "Unless we educate our immigrants they will be our ruin". Also, those living and working in urban centers wanted more public schools as a way of integrating the children of wealthy families with the children of middle class Americans. In spite of this pressure to form more public schools there were negative reactions to government funded schools:

1. Taxpayers worried that public education would result in higher taxes that would take money out of the pockets of the working class to fund education for the rich.

2. Churches felt that public schools would fail to teach religion sufficiently, especially as prejudice towards immigrants and Catholics grew in urban areas.

3. Private school teachers feared they would lose their jobs.

It was not until the 1840s that a structured system of public education came to the United States. Reformers built common schools state-by-state and promoted educational reform as a means to improve educational opportunity for all Americans. Common school reforms sought to establish completely free elementary schools available to all American children regardless of class, religion or economic condition.

Horace Mann was the major voice of educational reform in the mid-nineteenth century. He advocated for universal public education. He saw this as a way to teach all children to be good citizens of the democracy. A member of the Whig Party, Mann won support for building public schools and most states adopted versions of the system he started in Massachusetts. Following the Civil War, universal public schooling began at the primary level in the South although it was separate by race. In the North and West, private schools, especially those religiously affiliated were looked upon as being un-American. This was primarily aimed at the Roman Catholic schools.

By the beginning of the twentieth century the separation of Church and State in the public schools was well established by law. In spite of the law, there was a great deal of turmoil in the large city schools populated mostly by immigrants, but the schools in rural areas were insulated from these conflicts. Outside the cities, the typical school of nineteenth century New York was a one room, one teacher school, in which students of all ages were taught. Larger villages might have an academy or seminary. Attendance was voluntary, but the great majority of children attended some part of the year. The older children attended during the winter months but were needed on the farms during the summer.

In Amenia, New York, The Indian Rock School operated from 1858, "A decade before, New York, following a broad education reform movement of the time, had issued standard plans for a rural one-room schoolhouse with separate entrances for boys and girls to a single open room inside. Many adopted stylistic features of the early gothic revival movement such as steeply pitched roofs and board and batten siding".

"Amenia built 12 such schools around the town. The one on Mygatt Road acquired the name Indian Rock from a nearby lookout supposedly used by the area's Native American tribes. In 1927 the school was closed as districts began to consolidate into larger, more permanent schools." Unfortunately, most of the rural schools had declining enrollments and local taxes were unable to sustain the operation of the school district. Eventually "state aid" was necessary to keep rural districts operating.

During the depression, most of the 1930s, schools were closed because of economic reasons. High school populations grew rapidly because students were compelled to stay in school due to the scarcity of available jobs. According to Victor Bondi, "The number of high school students between 1930-1940 increased from 4.4 million to 6.5 million, straining the resources of financially strapped schools." Some educators suggested that high school graduation be made compulsory as a way of keeping young people out of the labor market. Other educators suggested lowering academic standards because so many new students were poorly prepared for classes.

Educational equality also had been high among the issues of educational concern during this time period. While generally accepted as a goal, equality had proven difficult to attain. The most noticed inequality was between students in the prosperous cities and those in the poorer rural districts. By the time the Depression started, New York State had over 10,000 school districts, of which over 8,000 had only a one room elementary school. Many communities could not afford more elaborate schools. Educational leaders argued that existing schools were not able to reach modern standards and that students from rural districts were lacking full educational opportunity. School consolidation was part of the solution proposed. Contosta and Cutler indicated, "The private or independent schools in Philadelphia came about to satisfy a need felt by wealthy white families to educate their children in a cultural and intellectual environment that would prepare them for the responsibilities befitting their gender, race and class status." This was true of the genesis of many of the private schools. Others came into existence due to religious convictions. Various Catholic ethnic groups such as the Irish, Italian and Polish, looked to parochial schools not only to protect their religion, but to enhance their culture and language.

The first parochial school in the United States was St. Mary's in Philadelphia in 1783. As the Catholic population expanded over the next 150 years, Catholic schools expanded at the same pace. Essential to this growth were the teaching orders of priests, sisters and brothers such as the Sisters of Charity, the Christian Brothers and the Jesuits to name a few.

Other religious dominations were also active in establishing church-related parochial schools. One of the reasons for this growth was the referendum based law in 1922 in the state of Oregon. This law required children between the ages of eight through sixteen to attend public school. The Supreme Court of the United States said the law was unconstitutional, affirming the right of private schools to exist and the right of parents to control the education of their children. Non-public schools began to sprout up more rapidly during the 1930s.

Christian Science is a set of beliefs and practices belonging to the metaphysical family of new religious movements. It was developed in 19th century New England by Mary Baker Eddy who wrote a book indicating sickness is an illusion that can be corrected by prayer alone. She named her book *Science and Health* and developed a large following by 1930. A census in 1936 found more than 250,000 Christian Scientists in the United States. Further, the church indicated there were more than 10,000 practitioner scientists trained to offer Christian Science prayer on behalf of others. Sunny Barlow was a practitioner who lived in New York City where she developed a sizable following of individuals who sought her services.

During the 1930s, the sleepy hamlet of Amenia was home to a unique religious retreat named Secret. The school was founded by Coral "Sunny" Barlow, a Christian Scientist (CS) practitioner living in New York City with her husband Bill Barlow and her brother Rex Armin. The 1930s witnessed the infamous Lindbergh kidnapping and many wealthy families were concerned about the safety of their children. In the years following the Lindbergh events, Sunny was encouraged, by some of her wealthier clients, to provide a retreat to learn/study/

work on Christian Science principles. In response to these urgings, she bought a farm in Amenia/Northeast, New York, which she transformed into a private, secluded boarding school, originally named Secret and later renamed Viewpoint. Two of her clients, Mrs. Worral Hyde and Mrs. George W. Merck, supported her efforts and became substantial benefactors.

Some of the children who attended Viewpoint possessed physical and/or cognitive disabilities. Sunny accepted these youngsters into her school with the hope of helping them through her Christian Scientist faith. One of the youngsters with a handicapping condition was John "Johnny" Merck, son of George and Serena Merck from New Jersey. Mrs. Merck was a devout woman who enrolled all three of her children in Viewpoint School.

Chapter 1

Aunt Marge

In 1943, Marge Heckel came to stay at Viewpoint with her friend and counselor, Sunny Barlow. Marge had just lost her husband due to illness. Still recovering from the loss, and in order to renew her faith, she decided to spend some time at Viewpoint with Sunny. Although she had no formal degrees or training, Sunny asked Marge to work with the handicapped students, caring for them and imparting whatever knowledge possible.

During the summer of 1943, Barbara Finger enrolled in Viewpoint. At that time, Barbara was going through a difficult period because her mother was quite ill and not expected to live much longer. Her father thought it best for her to live under the care and guidance of Sunny Barlow. She recalls, "Viewpoint provided me with a caring world and a fantastic education." Since it was a very small private school and Barbara was the only student taking the advanced math and Latin classes, for all practical purposes she was being tutored in those subjects. According to Barbara, in addition to a quality scholastic curriculum, Viewpoint offered tennis, horseback riding, and speech lessons. Looking back on her experience from a current prospective, Barbara hesitates to describe Viewpoint as a "prep" school, for it also became a safe place for several disabled students for whom other placements were not available in those days. This led to a student body comprised of a few disabled students, along with a larger group very qualified to attend college. She recalls the senior class of 1942 consisted of Serena "Bambi" Merck, Hester Pinchon, and Francis Lake, among others.

Sunny's Christian Scientist practice also served the purpose of recruiting students to Viewpoint. As word of her works became more widely dispersed, the student body became more diverse. In 1943 Chang Nai Kim, or "Chum" as he was called, was the lone male in the graduating class. Chum's family was part of a group of intellectuals who had fled Korea during the tumultuous times of the Second World War and Japanese occupation. Later, his two sisters came to Amenia and lived with their mother in a nearby farmhouse also owned by Sunny. Barbara was in the class of 1947 along with Joyce White, Joan Dean and Sally Funk.

As Viewpoint increased the size of the student body, there was some pressure placed on the school to become "accredited" by New York State. Also, when prospective families visited the school to explore possible enrollment for their child, some were taken aback by the presence of handicapped students. This created a second pressure point for Sunny to deal with – ending the care and teaching of the handicapped students.

During this time, Marge had become an excellent caregiver and educator to these students and would take them for a ride in the country whenever prospective students were visiting the school. Although an effective way to deal with one of Sunny's "pressures", this was merely a temporary solution. Marge grew to enjoy working with these youngsters and became an advocate for them. She felt that they could be happy and have a productive life living on a farm and doing the simple tasks required for independence. Serena Merck was delighted with Viewpoint and felt Johnny was in the "right " place under the care of Marge along with the prayers and support of Sunny. Her two daughters, Judith and Serena, were also enrolled at Viewpoint. Both were very active and prospered under Sunny's careful eye. Julian Strauss, an Amenia youngster, lived just down the street from Viewpoint and, as a day student, attended the lower grades. He remembers young Serena, who had acquired the name Bambi from her grandmother, as the prettiest girl in the school and a polite, very bright friend. The girls rather enjoyed the boarding school life, while their parents felt they were safe and in the capable hands of a very moral women.

The autumn of 1944 was noteworthy for several reasons including the baseball world, which was treated to an all St. Louis World Series. The mighty Cardinals, with Stan "The Man" Musial, were being challenged by the lowly Browns, their cross-town rivals featuring Pete Gray, a one-armed right fielder. As the year moved to a close, these three women decided to start a boarding school for youngsters who learn differently and might also possess physical handicaps. Sunny Barlow would provide the educational guidance, Marge Finger would provide the nurturing care, and Serena Merck would provide the bulk of the finances necessary for such a venture. As the year 1945 started, the women searched for an ideal location for their very special school. They probably didn't realize it at the time, but their school would be only the second boarding school for students with learning disabilities in New York state. The first was the Gow School located near Buffalo, New York, which was founded in 1925 and served students with dyslexia.

The Thompson Farm, leased by Ed Thompson from Rex Armin, was primarily a chicken farm. Since the economics for farmers were poor in the Hudson Valley during the war years, Ed Thompson decided to downsize his farm by no longer leasing 12 acres of his land located on the west side of Route 22 in Amenia. There was a farmhouse and several barns on the property. When Sunny Barlow found out from her brother the land and buildings were for sale, she must have been uncontrollably excited, and after discussing it with Marge, they informed Mrs. Merck. It was perfect: the farmhouse would be both the dining hall and the residence hall for all, and the barns could be converted into classroom space. It was also located close to Viewpoint, so Sunny could oversee everything. Best of all, the children would be safe and receive proper schooling in etiquette, practical skills, reading, writing and arithmetic.

The three founders were surely excited over the prospect of starting a program for the handicapped students living at Viewpoint. They consulted with each other, as well as some parents with children with handicapping conditions, and from these conversations, they determined what needed to be done to convert the farmhouse and other structures. Sunny hired some local carpenters to do the work and she and Marge made sure all the work was being done according to plan. John Finger was one of the local men working on this project. He was married with a teenage daughter and a very sick wife, and really became involved with the restoration project. John's wife passed away peacefully in 1944 and his daughter, Barbara, became deeply involved in Viewpoint. She, as a new student, and he, as a craftsman, were preparing for the opening of a new and exciting school. They both became very friendly with Marge, who could empathize with John since she had recently lost her husband. She also took an immediate liking to Barbara, who became very distraught when her mother was nearing the end. All three were sure that God would help them through their time of sorrow and near despair. As work progressed on readying Maplebrook Farm for the arrival of the first eight students in September 1945, the three founders agreed on the basic philosophy and curriculum of the school. The new school would emphasize good manners, faith in God, basic self-help skills, and practical academics. Marge would be the director of the school, while Sunny would be available for support and guidance at her campus two miles up the road. Eight students moved to the new campus and took up residence among eleven employees, including Marge Heckel and John Finger. The first bi-weekly payroll was issued in 1945 and totaled $287.50.

Marjorie (Marge) Heckel, although the Director of Maplebrook Farm, chose to be known as "Aunt Marge" by the Maplebrook community, and was the virtual heart and soul of the school. She brought more than just "book learning" to the daily life of the students. In providing a home away from home, her school became a challenging family environment. In this cozy atmosphere, teachers and staff sat interspersed with students in the dining hall at mealtime (a practice that continues today almost seventy-five years later). Sunny would visit Marge on Sundays and there would be singing and reading from the Good Book (*Science and Health by Mary Baker Eddy*). One Sunday per month, Marge would have the girls serve tea to Sunny and the others with all the proper etiquette observed. The tradition of no elbows on the table started with Sunny at Viewpoint and was brought to Maplebrook by Aunt Marge. The emphasis on work and manners were other "carry-overs" from Viewpoint. Maplebrook students received extensive training in achieving the social graces. Weekly classes included "posture and charm," speech and conversation, ballroom dancing, and a Saturday evening social followed by refreshments in the Girl's House.

Marge Heckel was a strong, determined woman who was dedicated to insuring Maplebrook Farm would be successful and have a positive impact on the eight students who lived there. She did everything: she taught, she cooked, she cleaned, she administered, she planned, and she did it all with little help. Then the inevitable happened after several years of working together, the widow, Marge and the widower, John decided to get married, and together they ran Maplebrook. Finances were always a big issue because they needed students to balance the budget. Sunny Barlow would help recruit students in New York City but Maplebrook Farm was not a recognized school and it was very difficult to convince parents to send their children to a school that was not recognized and approved by the state. In order to become a New York State chartered school, Marge had to recruit a Board of Trustees, elect officers, and apply to the New York State Board of Regents. In 1951, after six years operating Maplebrook Farm, a Board of trustees was established with Dorothy Marshall Barres, Serena S. Merck, Marjorie Finger, Katherine Hyde and John Grant serving as the first trustees. They met in Poughkeepsie in December 1951 at the Office of James T. Aspbury to form the corporation that would apply to New York for a charter for Maplebrook School. Mrs. Finger was elected President and Treasurer and Mrs. Hyde was elected as Vice-President and Secretary. It was at that first meeting they resolved to purchase the property and buildings on the west side of Route 22 from Mr. Rex Armin. Marge had been renting that property since 1945. Mr. Armin along with his sister, Sunny Barlow, founded the Viewpoint School in 1940. A 1956 obituary described Mr. Armin as follows:

> *Rex Kenneth Armin, 59, a founder of the Viewpoint School, Amenia, 16 years ago and president of the board of trustees of the school, died in the Sharon Hospital, Sharon, Conn., yesterday. He had been ill the last three months and had entered the hospital, Tuesday.*
>
> *Mr. Armin who was born in Waukesha, WI., Jan.11, 1887, was in the banking business in New York City for several years prior to founding the Amenia School and making his home there.*
>
> *The Son of the late Charles Eldridge and Florence Butterfield Armin, Mr. Armin's father was a judge in the*

criminal courts of Waukesha for some time. His Uncle, Charles Eldridge was in Congress for more than 30 years. Mr. Armin was graduated from Carroll College in Waukesha. He was a member of the Amity Club of Amenia and of the Peekskill Masonic Lodge.

Surviving, are his wife, Mrs. Norma Thompson Armin, whom he married in Yonkers, Nov. 28, 1931 and a sister, Mrs. Coral A. Armin Barlow of Amenia and New York City, who was a co-founder.

The Trustees dealt with supporting Aunt Marge but with meager finances. Substantial gifts from Mrs. Merck and Mrs. Hyde kept the school going during these early years.

Aunt Marge crafted a well-rounded learning experience for the students of Maplebrook School and the student body slowly grew to twenty students. Maplebrook received its provisional charter in 1951 and was approved by the state to award diplomas. An article in the Poughkeepsie Journal described the June 1956 graduation as such:

On June 9, Maplebrook School, Amenia, conducted commencement exercise, graduating four students from the eighth grade.

Those receiving diplomas were Penelope Cole, Brooklyn; Leslie Gay Heaton, Lynbrook; Virginia Rae Mason, Brooklyn; and Evelyn Sheffield Thompson, Atlanta, GA.

A buffet supper was served at the boys' annex for 80 parents and guests.

Speeches were made by the graduates. Mrs. John Finger, the director, gave the address to the graduates. Mrs.

C.A. Barlow presented the diplomas and Mrs. Gertrude Foley, principal of Maplebrook, awarded the prizes.

After the speeches and presentation of diplomas and awards, the Maplebrook choir, under the direction of Miss Clarice K. Neilson, sang several songs.

Maplebrook is opening for the summer session on July 6 for two months.

As you can see, in ten years Maplebrook Farm developed into a full range boarding school with festive graduations, choirs, awards and student speeches. This was the result of the determination and resilience possessed by Marge Finger. During these early formative years, Marge was the champion of the school. She taught, cooked, planned activities for students, guided faculty and staff and participated in developing an effective Board of Trustees that helped lead Maplebrook School in receiving a charter from the Board of Regents of The State of New York.

There were frequent times that the board received requests from Marge for more assistance as the school slowly became larger. Unfortunately, they didn't have the financial means to grant all of her requests so she had to press on with few supports. She did so with great skill and love of her job. She possessed a magic touch when it came to dealing with the students: Jerry Rossman, parent of Peter, class of '76, described his first visit to Maplebrook in 1970 as follows:

My wife Eva and I had been looking for a school for our son Peter for several years. We knew he had learning issues but did not know exactly what his learning problem was. We consulted with various psychologists and educators who recommended schools in the "country" located in New Jersey or upstate New York. We were shocked when

we visited the schools because they were more like insti-
tutions and appeared cold and impersonal. We then con-
sulted with Dr. Harold Michael-Smith who worked for
the Association for Help of Retarded Children (AHRC) in
New York City who told us Peter has some similarities as
the children AHRC served but was not mentally retarded,
he just learned differently. He went on to say that he had
heard of a small boarding school upstate in Amenia that
might be a good match for Peter and suggested we visit it.

It was a sunny day when Eva and Jerry brought Peter to Maplebrook to meet Marge Finger (Aunt Marge). The three of them walked into her office and were greeted by a large smile and reassuring words that immediately put them at ease except for Peter who was a bit apprehensive. Marge sensed Peter's feelings and suggested she and Peter take a walk around campus to see the facilities. Jerry went on to say, "Marge put her arm on Peter's shoulder and they walked away from the office and Peter fell in love with Maplebrook". Marge Finger worked her magic and made Peter feel comfortable.

Not only did Aunt Marge work her "magic" with the students and their parents, but she was also a very capable administrator. In her annual report to the Trustees in 1956, Marge Finger stated, "all indications point to the fact that Maplebrook School is definitely a growing enterprise. Last fall we began our school year with twenty-five residents and one day student. In June, we graduated four girls from eighth grade with accredited diplomas. Of these, one has returned for a post-graduate course and is furthering her vocational aptitude of perhaps being a trainer in an obedience school for dogs". Even as she was helping Maplebrook School to grow, Marge had the insight to see the importance of postsecondary vocational training for some of the students. Her annual report went on to say:

"we are again permitted to use the Webutuck School gym in Amenia for $10.00 per night until such time as we can financially provide a gym of our own. Your president cannot stress too emphatically this urgent need. We have a more active group and without a gym and a recreational director, our problem is clear. The acquisition of a gym would definitely lessen pressures on our staff in general. This improvement to our plant would make it more attractive for future applicants, both students and high caliber staff." Aunt Sunny" continues to do excellent work in her classes in ethics and sees the children in groups and individually when there is a need." "There is very much activity in our scholastic field. On the average of three inquiries come each week and this is a portent of the future." "Our enrollment at the present time is fourteen girls and fourteen boys and two girl day students. Our staff is essentially the same. Mrs. Banks, my assistant, arrived in September. Her potentiality is great but it is too early to state that she can apply it to our benefit. She is sincere and very eager to carry out the duties which relieve me for more personal work with the children."

Marge Finger possessed a vision of what Maplebrook could become by filling an important niche in the education available to youngsters who learned differently. In December of 1956, Coral "Sunny" Barlow passed away and Marge lost a friend and a mentor. An editorial in the Maplebrook News, the campus newspaper, read as follows: "This issue of the news is being dedicated to our "Aunt Sunny", She always taught us, death is just a step into another grade. Those of us who were privileged to know her in close association feel she is still guiding, governing and protecting us each day."

"The lives she has touched are all the better for having known her. As the dedication sheet so aptly states, she drew a circle that let him in. To "Aunt Sunny" each one of us has potentialities of being useful, God loving individuals. In her heart she never turned away anyone. All God's children are worthy of the highest effort of teachability. In the spring, Maplebrook students, faculty and staff are planting a row of dogwood trees on each side of the walk going out to the schoolhouse. Every Monday, when Sunny and I would leave the girls dorm to go to her class in ethics, she would stop, reach for my arm and say, "Jewel, I can't get over how beautiful this place looks and what wonderful opportunities for service are manifested at Maplebrook." What better way could we continually be reminded of the purpose of our school than to have a living memorial to "Aunt Sunny."

Marge continued to press forward in her multiple roles of President of the Board of Trustees and Executive Director (Head) of the School. It was around this time that Marge learned that the twenty-five acre Thompson chicken farm was going to be offered for sale. The farm was located directly across Route 22 from Maplebrook and would be ideal for the expansion Marge envisioned. She convinced the Trustees to buy the farm with the idea of building a new gym on the property, remodeling the chicken barn into the classroom space and converting the large farmhouse into a girls dormitory. To complete all this and purchase the twenty-five acre farm, Marge convinced several of the Trustees to lend Maplebrook money. She and John lent the school considerable funds to help in this effort.

Under the guidance of Marge Finger and a very committed Board of Trustees, Maplebrook School's enrollments grew from eight in its inaugural year, 1945, to thirty-two students in 1957. Staff grew to include several teachers, a psychologist and a recreation director. In addition, Maplebrook was developing a more traditional schedule of classes. In her 1957 Annual Report to the Trustees she indicates:

> *"Because we are enrolling youngsters who are more ready for longer scholastic periods, I am recommending to the Board that we have classes on Monday for school work. The co- curricular activities can be shifted to other periods during the week. In regular schools, art and music periods are done during school hours. They are taken in the classroom and teachers do planning work, etc., during this time. With classes five days a week, plus the many very important co-curricular activities, Maplebrook will indeed have a well- rounded program." She goes on to say, "from the amount of inquiries coming in each week asking about our program at Maplebrook, it appears we are acquiring a fine reputation."*

As Maplebrook was growing in both size and reputation, the important question of support for Marge Finger was more difficult to solve. The Board minutes of 1957 indicate, "the experiment of having Mrs. Banks as an assistant has not been satisfactory. We have been very fortunate in securing the services of Mrs. Leona Tompkins who is doing a fine piece of work in the office and could readily serve as an assistant. She has great understanding of our set up and her approach to parents awaiting my arrival in the office has been most satisfactory." During the 1950s, one of the biggest sources of support for Marge Finger was Mr. John S. Grant who was a member of the Board of Trustees and worked as business manager since April 1957. Mr. Grant was especially helpful in planning the expansion of Maplebrook's physical plant. He also helped in the identification and solicitation of charitable foundations who might assist Maplebrook in some of their future projects. Mr. Grant, who had been friendly with Rex Armin when he was

WHERE DREAMS COME TRUE

guiding Viewpoint School, felt it may be important for parents to form a Parents' Association to discuss issues and concerns. One of the important issues that weighed on the thoughts of parents was what would happen with their children after completion of Maplebrook's academic program. This Parents' Association would slowly grow and have a far reaching impact on the pace and direction of special education in the 1970s at MBS.

Maplebrook was beginning to experience a slight change in its population as indicated by the October 1957 Annual Report where Marge Finger indicated, "This past year at Maplebrook has been one of growth in every aspect of development. We are attracting a very different type of student as to a greater degree of teachability. Since the term began, I can truthfully say that there is no student enrolled who should not be at Maplebrook. Apparently, our screening process is efficiently done plus the experience gained from insisting on a more complete past history, medically and scholastically."

Maplebrook was experiencing growing pains in that the full complement of students needed more facilities for study and sports. For many years Maplebrook was able to use the gymnasium at the Webutuck School in Amenia for a small fee. As the Webutuck School grew they needed to convert their gym to a cafeteria and Maplebrook was without a gymnasium. Mr. Grant, also known as "Daddy" Grant and Mrs. Finger presented a plan to the trustees to enlarge the schoolhouse, and after that was completed, to initiate the process of planning and building a gymnasium. In October of 1957 Mrs. Finger told the trustees that Maplebrook could not use the Webutuck gymnasium and, "therefore, a building that can be used for gymnastics, games, dancing and basketball practice is desperately needed, especially to give our recreational director, who has proven his ability along these lines, a place to carry out his excellent program."

In 1958 Mrs. Finger met with the trustees to tour the facilities at Maplebrook. She mentioned that she had received many suggestions to identify the new recreational facility with the name of the school's great benefactor, the late George W. Merck. She advised the trustees that she had informally spoken with Mrs. Merck regarding naming the new gymnasium Merck Hall. The trustees were in agreement and also gave thanks to Mr. Grant for the thought and work he had done in the construction of this new facility. George W. Merck was born in New York City in 1894. His father had emigrated from Germany in 1891 to oversee the new office of E. Merck and Company. He was raised in New Jersey and graduated from Harvard College with a BS in Chemistry. World War I prevented him from pursuing an advanced degree so he joined his father at the Merck Company. He was made President of the company in 1925, shortly before his father's death. He oversaw Merck's involvement in the development of synthetic vitamins, sulfas, antibiotics, and hormones. During World War II he led the war research service, which initiated the U.S. biological weapons program. He was on the cover of Time Magazine on August 18, 1952. George Merck was a tower of a man standing 6' 5" and had a variety of philanthropic causes. He and his wife, Serena, were major benefactors of Maplebrook School.

In her annual report given to the trustees in May, 1958, Mrs. Finger told the board:

> At present time, Maplebrook has an enrollment of thirty-four boarding students and two day students. The group consists of sixteen girls and eighteen boys and two girl day students. We are really crowded in both girls' and boys' dorms. The congestion in the boys dorm was somewhat alleviated by placing two boys over the workshop in the room which was formerly the office. Mr. Tadd supervises these boys. An ideal situation would be to finish off the

WHERE DREAMS COME TRUE

remaining half of the upstairs to enable the staff member to have his room and the boys use Mr. Tadd's apartment as well as the former office. Mr. Grant states that this need not be a prohibitive step financially as much of the work can be done by the maintenance department. We have a waiting list for the girls and could have placed three boys if we were to increase our enrollment. With our present staff and facilities this is not feasible. Inquiries continue to arrive on the average of three a week. Word of mouth reference to Maplebrook seems to be quite active. Apparently, we are establishing a satisfactory reputation for which we may all be proud. Our supervisor from Albany visited Maplebrook recently and was greatly impressed with all the improvements since his last visit two years ago. In Maplebrook's history, nothing equals the wonderful asset of having our junior gym. With this more active group, plus having a place for our recreational director to function, it was essential and has been a joy to the students and staff. It is amazing how we ever were able to carry out our busy schedule without this addition. We held our Speech banquet there on April 26th and the comments of parents and friends were most gratifying. Our student group wishes me to personally thank the Board of Trustees for this fine addition to our physical set up."

With the physical plant expanded to meet the needs to thirty six students enrolled at the school, Mr. Grant and Mrs. Finger asked the trustees for permission to apply to the New York State Board of Regents for an absolute charter. The October 1958 minutes indicate the following resolution:

"Whereas, Maplebrook School has been operating under an extension of the provisional charter granted on the 30th

day of November 1956, which authorized the applica-
tion for a permanent charter at the expiration of the three
year period and, whereas, the Trustees are satisfied that
they can offer to the Regents evidence that the Institution
possesses equipment available for its use and support, and
sufficient for its charter purposes, and maintain an or-
ganization of usefulness and character satisfactory to the
Regents to warrant the granting of an absolute charter. Be
it therefore resolved, that the Board of Regents be requested
to replace the provisional charter of Maplebrook School by
an absolute charter"

Thus, in a bit more than ten years, Marge Finger, an individual driven by faith and with no formal training in education, was able to lead Maplebrook from a safe haven for a few handicapped children to a fine school for youngsters who learned differently that was recognized by the state of New York. She was able to do this by sheer determination, hard work, and the support and guidance of an exceptional Board of Trustees led by John Grant, Katherine Hyde and Serena Merck.

Since its founding in 1945, Maplebrook had been driven by the will and faith of one person and, by 1960, Marge Finger felt herself slowing down and realized that she needed help. She had received assistance from dedicated board members like John Grant during the 1950s but she knew she had to find an assistant with the dedication and resolve necessary to increase the school's educational quality while extending its physical plant.

During the early 1960s Marge Finger continued to be the heart and soul of the school. Betty Howes and her husband Dick were searching for a school for their son Rick. When they visited Maplebrook and met "Aunt Marge" they knew they had found the perfect setting for Rick to thrive. Rick remembered "Aunt Marge" as a kind, understanding woman who was strict but loving. "She always encouraged me and made sure I would succeed on any task I started. She was a wonderful woman who showed us she cared." Rick remembered at an alumni reunion in the 1980s. He and his roommate Rodrick Wilson remembered doing calisthenics each morning before school on the field near the schoolhouse. Betty and Dick were from Cincinnati, Ohio but bought a house in Sharon, CT to be near Rick and they volunteered to help out at the school. In October 1962, Richard (Dick) Howes became a member of the Board of Trustees and began more than 30 years of service to the before school. Dick Howes was born in Middleboro, Mass., and was a graduate of Worcester Polytechnic Institute and he saw active duty in World War II as an officer in the Navy. Dick worked in the valve business for 27 years. He was vice –president of marketing for the Lunkenheimer Company in Cincinnati, Ohio before retiring in 1973. He was proud to say that his family was of very old New England stock and he was a member of the Society of Mayflower descendants. He was president of Mid-County little league for many years and served on the Board at the Sharon Country Club and was a member of the Sharon Planning and Zoning commission. He held many volunteer positions at Maplebrook School at the Board level and served as acting Headmaster as well as business manager at the school. At that time, The Maplebrook School campus was divided by Route 22. The boys lived in the original farmhouse on the west side of Route 22 and the girls lived in the newly purchased Thompson Farmhouse on the east side of Route 22. The students named the boys' residence the Maples and the girls' residence Brook House.

That year the Deputy Commissioner of Mental Hygiene visited Maplebrook and indicated, "he was happy to be able to report back to the department that we were running a school for young people having IQs of 70 and above and not one for mental defectives." This report solidified Maplebrook's mission of providing education for slow learners and youngsters who learn differently.

Student enrollments were holding steady at forty students, twenty girls and twenty boys, with a waiting list. The trustees were planning for expansion of the schoolhouse and dorms in order to increase the student body. They also realized the importance of obtaining an assistant for "Aunt Marge", so Dick Howes "kindly undertook to go to Columbia University to inquire about a possible understudy for Mrs. Finger". While the school searched for an understudy, Marge Finger made the following presentation to the entire Maplebrook community in the fall of 1963. She entitled the speech "Brains and Brawn" and stated the following:

> "Merck Hall – presented to Maplebrook School in 1959 by Mr. and Mrs. George Merck, established the name and reason for this present occasion. Maplebrook has been more fortunate in its friends and trustees. In a recent issue of the New York Times, I read that a gift of one million dollars to Columbia University was to apply to the construction of a gymnasium – total cost of which will be about nine million dollars. If justification for such an amount is the value of a gym to the student body at Columbia, you may well grasp the asset Merck Hall has been to Maplebrook since 1959. A small but enduring record of our gratitude to Mr. and Mrs. George Merck is the name given to our gymnasium, "Merck Hall".

> In 1962, an addition and alteration of our ancient schoolhouse was completed. It is a thing of beauty and efficiency; its impact on our faculty and students was inspiring. The new school was dedicated to students past and present who helped us build Maplebrook.

> With "Brains" taken care of by the enlarged schoolhouse, it became obvious that "Brawn" must be taken care of

with an enlarged gym. Once more the practical interest of Maplebrook's friends and trustees provided the means and ways to expand Merck Hall. On June 16, 1963, excavation began; by July 1st foundations were ready for Mr. Leon Cheseboro and his team of carpenters to begin construction, delivering the completed gym in 60 days. Finishing and painting has been completed plus landscaping. Basketball equipment, etc. is now being installed. Merck Hall had 1200 square feet of floor space. Today, it has 4000 square feet of playing floor plus a real, honest-to-goodness dramatic stage with dressing rooms on an additional 500 square feet. If Columbia's gym has a floor like this one, it's their good luck. This maple floor, laid and finished is a special gift from Mrs. Rosalie Cramer, one of our much loved trustees.

Now – we may cavort – roller skate – or play ball or Sarah Bernhardt to our soul's content in the ample new gym. "Merck Hall" dedicated to the physical fitness and good sportsmanship of Maplebrook's students; present, and in years to come, with the love and good wishes of our trustees.

Marjorie H. Finger, Director

In 1964, the school finally hired support for the hard working Marge Finger. Mr. Robert Hiltenbrand was hired as principal and the trustees agreed to Marge's recommendation that the student enrollment be brought to fifty students. To accommodate Mr. Hiltenbrand and his family, they built a four bedroom 2,000 square foot house east of Brook House and south of the expanded schoolhouse. As stated in the May 1964 Board minutes: "Be it resolved Robert Hiltenbrand joined our faculty on July 1st. Assuming the role of principal, he is in complete charge of the education program at Maplebrook, including the appointment or dismissal of teachers. He has taken over this position well and has relieved your president of many duties." The education program continued to grow in both size and quality. Teachers were added in academic subjects as well as horsemanship. A 4H forget-me-not club was established as part of student activities and developed an outstanding reputation in Dutchess County winning many awards. It was in 1964 that the first alumni association was established with John Treadway as President, Carol Swartz as Secretary and Harry Barnes as Treasurer.

All Board members were spreading the word to their friends regarding the outstanding work being done at the Maplebrook campus. Dick and Betty Howes had made the acquaintance of Dr. Roger Moore since their arrival in Sharon, CT. Dr. Moore was very involved with establishing the Sharon Clinic, the precursor to Sharon Hospital. Marge Finger was involved with the Amenia Grange, the Amenia Volunteer Fire Department, and a variety of civic groups. Mr. Grant was able to keep up with new state education initiatives and Mr. Howes worked to insure the budget was adequate for the growing school. All seemed to be going according to plans in 1964. Enrollments were strong, the educational program was expanding and the school was developing a noteworthy reputation. Also in 1964 the students chose Woodcliff as the name of the house built for the principal. In October 1965 Marge announced to the board that Robert Hiltenbrand tendered his resignation in August. With the help of Barbara Toner, her stepdaughter, "Aunt Marge" hired Harry N. Rusack as the new principal. It was also in 1965 that the tradition of alumni attending the prom in May started. Twenty eight alumni came back from distances including Maine and Wisconsin to visit their alma mater.

As the school continued to grow, the fact that Route 22 separated the boys dorm (The Maples) from the main campus began to be problematic. The school needed to expand because they needed a larger dining hall, more room for boys, a music room and a reception room. Marge ably guided these thoughts along with Mr. Grant and together they developed plans for what is now Fazzone Hall and Evans Hall. But before construction could be done on those facilities, it was necessary for preliminary work to be done on the water system and the campus roadway. Also change was on its way in other areas as "Aunt Marge" announced that Mabelle McKinney and Calvin Gardner, after years in charge of cooking, would be retiring as of June 15th.

The Samara yearbook was established in 1966 under the guidance and watchful eye of "Aunt Marge" and several teachers along with the volunteer efforts of Bettina Howes. This was another small step in enabling Maplebrook to have all the amenities as other private schools. Even as there were small positive changes for the fledgling school, there were system issues that needed to be resolved. First and foremost was the need to build a support system for Marge Finger including an assistant director. Second, was to affect some stability of staff, Third was to insure enrollments remained steady and finally, to build a strong board of trustees committed to working towards realizing the mission of the school.

Harry Barnes, on a visit to campus in 1990, described Maplebrook as the perfect place to go to school. All the students were friendly and the teachers were demanding but kind and understanding. Harry remembered being friendly with John Finger and being allowed to help with some maintenance and small repair projects. Harry remarked that Aunt Marge was in charge of everything. She knew everything about the schoolhouse program and what was going on in the dorms. Harry loved it here and met his wife, who was also a student, while at Maplebrook. John Treadway became a cook at Williams College in Williamstown and credited Maplebrook for helping him be prepared to hold a job and getting along with others. The alumni enjoyed returning to campus and touching base with Uncle Gus (Gustave Diester), Uncle

John (John Finger), Aunt Lee (Leona Waldorph), and Aunt Margaret (Margaret Diester). The 1960s were a turbulent time at many college and high school campuses, but Maplebrook was insulated by the warm feelings created by Aunt Marge and her staff.

The 1960s were also a time of change and that was very true for Maplebrook as Lee Waldorph, who had worked as Aunt Marge's secretary since the early 1950s, resigned and left Maplebrook. Mrs. Waldorph was frequently the first Maplebrook staff member prospective students met when they and their parents visited Maplebrook. She would greet the visitors and make sure they were comfortably settled outside "Aunt Marge's" office and chat with them until "Aunt Marge" was prepared to meet them. Lee Waldorph was also board secretary and when she resigned in 1968, Margaret Deister was elected to replace her. In 1968 John Finger passed away after a short illness. John had been a huge source of support, for Aunt Marge along with John Grant. This was a terrible blow to Aunt Marge and she repeatedly asked the trustees to find an assistant for her. Staff and faculty who knew "Aunt Marge" during this time observed she was visibly shaken by John's death and she seemed to slow down a bit in the years that followed. Around this time Dick Howes' efforts to find an assistant for "Aunt Marge" was rewarded and he hired Richard Snyder as principal. Dick Howes was of the opinion that "Aunt Marge" needed an educator to act as principal and John Grant would be able to assist Marge with the financial aspects of the school. This worked out well for a few years and the Board of Trustees was supportive as they pondered whether to accept a contract to obtain students through New York State and to increase teacher/staff salaries because of the relatively high salaries given by the neighboring Wassaic State School.

John Grant, who had been a board member since the beginning, realized that the Board of Trustees needed to be enlarged. He asked the trustees to recommend persons of resolve and character to join the

Board of Trustees. In October of 1969, Mary Babcock from Sharon, CT, visited the school and was impressed with the education taking place on the small quaint campus. She expressed interest in joining the board and was elected in April of 1970. This was the same month and year as the Apollo 13 moon landing. As the crew on the Apollo 13 was battling adversity so were the Maplebrook trustees. They were celebrating their 25th anniversary, the opening of a new boys' dormitory, a new kitchen and dining hall, and a student body of fifty students. In addition to running the school, Marge was also the president of the Board of Trustees. This was a tremendous burden for a small tired woman in her sixties. The board at this time established a management committee to help Marge with some of the weighty decisions that plagued her at the time. Unfortunately, just as she was getting more help, she lost her main support when John "Daddy" Grant died in 1971.

Chapter 2

———∿∿———

MR. MAPLEBROOK

SHORTLY THEREAFTER A young man from the Midwest visited Maplebrook in response to an advertisement for a principal that was posted at the placement office at Ball State University in Indiana. Lonnie Adams was very surprised when he stepped on the Maplebrook campus. He was surprised at the size of Amenia. He, his wife Judy and two daughters grew to love the town in their almost eighteen years at Maplebrook. Lonnie Adams was hired as principal in 1971 and immediately recognized that some work needed to be done to modernize the curriculum. He started to shape a progressive and supportive course of study for the students at Maplebrook. Marge was pleased to have some assistance in doing the everyday tasks needed to conduct a smooth running, efficient boarding school. This way she could spend more time building a board and watching over all the children enrolled at the school.

Several parents of students were quite active and were putting pressure on the board to make some changes in the delivery of services at the School. Mrs. Rosalie Hurst and Mr. Jerome I. Rossman, Jr. were two of the most active parents. Marge thought their energy and activism could be of use on the Board of Trustees. So Marge nominated them for membership on the board. At the same time, she resigned as president of the Board of Trustees and Dr. Roger Moore was elected board president. The new board decided that a major reorganization would be helpful to advance the school and give some much needed assistance to Aunt Marge. Dick Howes would be in charge of the business office with help from Margaret Deister and Lon Adams would be in charge of all academics and academic support services like speech therapy, tutoring and counselling. The management committee would pitch in to help when they thought it necessary. Perhaps the largest support for the school was given by the Merck family. Board minutes indicate many substantial monetary gifts throughout the 1960s and 1970s. Most of these were used for various building projects or to erase deficits. One of the largest gifts was that of Windridge, the house the Merck family built for Johnnie Merck when he was one of the original eight students, when the school started in 1945. This spacious house, with an attached servants quarters, had stood vacant since Johnnie's medical issues necessitated his moving to a facility where his medical needs could be met. Serena Merck was the driving force behind the early days of Maplebrook. In the 1970s Maplebrook was moving into new phases of its development with an educator who placed a new emphasis on the academic program while maintaining many of the traditions established by "Aunt Marge". The minutes from the October 2, 1973 board meeting describes the "new" organization of Maplebrook as follows:

The following nominations were presented:

> *President – Dr. Roger W. Moore*
> *Vice-President – Mrs. Mary S. Babcock*
> *Secretary – Treasurer – Mrs. Margaret Y. Deister*

There being no further nominations and on a motion made by Mr.

Arthur White, and seconded by Mr. Charles Razee, it was unanimously carried that the Secretary cast one ballot for the slate as presented.

After discussion, proper motions were made, seconded and approved that the following committees be in order:

Executive Committee: Mrs. Rosalie H. Hurst, Chairman
Mr. Jerome I. Rossman, Jr.
Mr. Arthur White
Alternates: Mrs. Serena S. Merck
Mrs. Mary S. Babcock

Planning and Finance Committee: Mr. Donald T. Warner,
Chairman
Mrs. Katherine L. Hyde
Mr. Jerome I. Rossman, Jr.
Mrs. Serena S. Merck
Mr. Everett Schultheis

Advisors and Consultants: Mrs. Margaret Deister, Treasurer
Mr. Leon Rothstein, Accountant
Mr. Richard S. Howes, Business
Administrator

Education and Admissions Committee: Mr. Arthur W. White,
Chairman
Mr. Edward W. Renfree
Mrs. Mary S. Babcock
Mrs. Rosalie H. Hurst
Mrs. Barbara Coggeshall
Mr. Jerome I. Rossman, Jr.
Mrs. Susan R. von Stade

Advisor: Mr. Lonnie L. Adams

<u>*Building and Grounds Committee*</u>*: Mr. Charles B. Razee,*
Chairman
Mr. Edward W. Renfree
Mrs. Mary S. Babcock
Mrs. Barbara Coggeshall
Mrs. Katherine L. Hyde

Dr. Roger W. Moore, President, is to be a member, ex-officio of each committee. Additions to the committees may be made as deemed necessary.

Perhaps one of the biggest changes that occurred in the 1970s had to do with Marge Finger's job title. Since 1945 Marge Finger had been the face of Maplebrook. She had been called the Executive Director, the President and the Head of School. She requested that since the business end of the school was in the capable hands of the Board of Trustees, she felt that she wished to devote all her time to student issues and requested her job title be changed to Dean of Students at the October 1973 meeting of the trustees. Marge Finger gave her first report as Dean of Students:

> *It is my pleasure to give the first report to the Board of Trustees as "Dean of Students".*
>
> *As is customary, you will require the present status of enrollment. The numbers of students enrolled at the present time are 19 boys and 26 girls – totaling 45 students. Unfortunately, this is low, but this seems to be the status of many private schools. We are receiving requests for*

Maplebrook material, on the average of one telephone call or letter a day. I personally feel that we will be taking in more students before the end of 1973-74 period. The Admissions Committee will give you the details as to sources of inquiries. Many of the letters and reports received contain information indicative of the fact the prospective student is definitely not qualified for enrollment at Maplebrook. Students presently on campus are from 14 states, Canada, Mexico and Beirut, Lebanon. The present student body is considerably better qualified than those here this past summer.

The committees represented by the Board of Trustees are most helpful and greatly appreciated.

As Dean of Students, my contact with the students is proving helpful, and being in charge of house parents and housekeepers is making for better teamwork and greater communications with each other. This is done with one thought in mind – that the students are our primary concern.

Several weeks ago, one of our students went to Mr. Howes to state that he was graduating in June 1974. To show his thanks for what Maplebrook had done for him these past four years, he wanted to volunteer his services next summer as a member of the maintenance staff. Mr. Howes thanked him for his great offer and stated he would receive a reply after the Board of Trustees met. In the meantime, we have advised his father of the matter and are anxious to receive word from him.

Our school teacher's requirements have been elevated.

WHERE DREAMS COME TRUE

Three new teachers have, or are going to school evenings to get, their Masters Degrees in Special Education. Our new cook is a senior at the Culinary Institute now located in Hyde Park, New York. His classes are so arranged that he is able to prepare breakfast and dinner before he leaves for his classes. He arranges for the supper meal, and his wife and student kitchen helpers assist in preparing the evening meal.

Dr. Roger Moore was first elected President of the Board of Trustees in 1973 and continued to lead Maplebrook through 1987. His thoughtful and scholarly approach to leadership was instrumental in moving Maplebrook forward to being one of the finest boarding schools of its kind. The 1974 President's Report illustrates Dr. Moore's recognition of Maplebrook's potential and of the key individuals who would help elevate this small school to become one of the best in New York State:

President's Report

May 24, 1974

This President's report will focus on three areas:

Firstly, the valid belief that we have a fine school in Maplebrook, a staff of outstanding teachers, and a physical plant that is equal to others. These facts were confirmed in the course of a short stay in New York City during the annual convention of the Council for Exceptional Children in mid-April. The booths and displays of other schools were barely, or not at all as impressive as that of Maplebrook. Visitors to our booth, including alumni, educational psychologists, therapists and educational consultants evinced a sincere interest in "How is Maplebrook doing" or "Where is Maplebrook?" Perhaps, most striking, was the great number of exhibitors, overflowing the available space of two hotels with their hardware and products all designed for special education, emphasizing again and again, that we are involved in a very big business. That, in itself, may give us pause: are we really in the big time......how do we rate in the big picture......are we doing the best we can in this field.....are we doing all we can to advertise and deliver our product. Incidentally one of our teachers, who had circulated among those from other parts of the country, was somewhat surprised, but enthusiastically reported that Maplebrook salaries were right up there with other comparable scales, at least within her circle of inquiries. Let's keep it that way.

Secondly, (and already mentioned) I want to underline the wisdom of Mr. Adams, in proposing the Woodcliff project. In New York, one consultant mentioned her regret that we had not (then) been able to accept some older students she had had in mind. She was, of course, referring to the after-high-school group; some of who needs at least Woodcliff proposes to fill. This is the kind of thinking (innovative) that marks a school such as Maplebrook as exceptional. For rather than detract from the more conventional classes and study planning, Woodcliff will undergird their value in supplying that training that the younger students need – and will always need – in preparation for the later and transitional years. The fact that we already have commitments for another year – or two – from students who ordinarily would be expected to leave us this June – before the program has even begun – should demonstrate the value of this particular effort and encourage us in the direction of like endeavors – the filling of needs heretofore not altogether realized.

Thirdly, a more complex consideration. We are, I think, agreed that this year, in many ways, has been a good one – particularly with respect to harmony, among and within echelons of student and administrative organization and function. Problems are always with us, but the hope I wish to certify is that we not, ever, rest on our laurels. Are there improvements that could be made? Do we have as efficient an administrative organization as we should? Are we utilizing all our talents?

WHERE DREAMS COME TRUE

Specifically, do our administrative officers have enough help? Does Mrs. Finger – Mr. Howes, Mrs. Deister – Mr. Adams - ? Are things being left undone that ought not to be left undone? Are the house parents doing a good job – do we need better ones? Is there enough social and personnel (not personal) supervision for the students? How are the weekends working out? Do we need more counseling, psychological or otherwise?

I think what I am trying to say is this: let us never again be caught looking the other – or the wrong way, as we were a few short years ago. The administration of a school is the core of its soul, its spirit – its failure, its success. To administrative officers we owe a great deal, especially as our present ones have given us so much. To this end, I propose that an <u>annual</u> *review of administrative policy and personnel be one of the first duties of both the Executive Committee and the Long Range Planning Committee. I further suggest that preliminary study be accomplished by each committee within the next 60 days, so that by mid-July they can submit a joint report to the Chairman of the Board, in prospect for possible changes, and in time for the 74-75 academic year.*

While I suspect that the committees will want to evaluate each administrative position individually as well as collectively, I leave the approach and method to the wisdom of the group. It is with this charge that the Chairman concludes his report, with thanks for your wholehearted support and backing through this recent year.

Respectfully submitted,

Roger W. Moore, M.D
President

Dr. Moore's vision and wisdom created the foundation for the Maplebrook leadership for decades. Mrs. Rosalie H. Hurst, chair of the

Executive Committee of the Board of Trustees, outlined the conditions for the retirement of "Aunt Marge". She reported, in August of 1974:

"For about the last ten years Marge Finger has been wanting help and our committee now feels Maplebrook is in a strong position. During the last couple of years Aunt Marge has been mentioning retirement. We believe we must face facts and realize she deserves retirement. The Executive Committee, therefore, recommends that we work with Mr. Adams in trying to find someone suitable to help him. More and more of Aunt Marge's duties should be apportioned to other members of the staff so she can "ease off". When we have found adequate help for Mr. Adams, Aunt Marge can then retire. Her life is and has been MAPLEBROOK since 1945. We would like her to feel Hilltop is her home as long as she wants to stay with us. She has expressed the desire of working closely with Alumni and we would be most grateful to her for helping us keep more adequate records. She is almost the mother to our alumni and we want all Maplebrook Alumni to have the benefit of her love and guidance."

Respectfully submitted,

Rosalie H. Hurst, Chairman

On October 18, 1974 Lonnie L. Adams was appointed the second headmaster of Maplebrook School and Marjorie H. Finger was appointed to be President Emeritus, consultant and in charge of Alumni Affairs.

The Executive Committee, chaired by Mary S. Babcock, decided it was time to start a new fund drive in order to build a new schoolhouse and indoor swimming pool. The additional classroom space was needed because as Lonnie Adams had indicated in his 1975 report to the Education Committee, "We feel the program would be greatly enhanced if we could reduce the number of students in a classroom from approximately eleven per class to perhaps eight per class". He went on to say , "The need for additional classroom and office space for faculty continues to have an adverse effect on our long range educational outlook". This progressive vision was indicative of the strong educational background Lonnie Adams possessed as the second headmaster of Maplebrook School. To bolster his staff and the new emphasis on academic quality, Lonnie Adams hired Mr. Dean Stickles for an administrative position as his assistant. The Adams-Stickles team kept the school moving forward as Dr. Moore wished. To increase quality in the classroom, Dr. Moore was concerned about staff appointments and suggested "periods of trial teaching" be explored. The October 1976 board minutes indicate all was going well and classroom quality was improving while Maplebrook experienced its fourth consecutive year operating "in the black."

Maplebrook was developing a reputation as a leader in educating students with learning challenges. In 1976 Lonnie Adams stated, "As I begin my fifth year of service to Maplebrook School, I would like to reflect on....the program is not only maintaining high standards set by Maplebrook over the years, but, is fast becoming a model for other special schools to follow. We have made Giant strides towards individualizing our remedial program and continue to upgrade our staff as vacancies occur." He also felt the addition of several part time psychologists by Dean Stickles not only helped the students, but also offered guidance and support to the faculty and staff. On May 21, 1977 the new schoolhouse was dedicated to John S. Grant and the new pool house was dedicated to Mrs. Marjorie H. Finger. Those 1977 minutes also indicated, "Mrs. Finger, President Emeritus, reported her rapport with the students is increasing as she goes to the dorms in the evenings to just talk with the students. She also enjoys having the students stay with her overnight at various times." This was truly a testament to her devotion to the Maplebrook student.

It was at this meeting that Public Law 94-142 was explained to the trustees. Dean Stickles attended a National Association of Private Schools for Exceptional Children (NAPSEC) Conference and explained to the trustees that this act required all public schools to provide equal access to education for children with physical and/or mental disabilities. Public schools were required to evaluate handicapped children and create an individualized education plan with parent input that would emulate as close as possible the educational experience of non-disabled students. Lonnie and Dean went on to say they were unsure of the impact this law would have on Maplebrook School. It could mean that parents unhappy with their local public school might be able to choose a private school and have the public school pay the tuition. Both suggested it would take five years to gauge the impact of the law. Dick Howes cautioned the financial aspects of the law were unclear as each state was developing their own guidelines.

As PL 94-142 shook up the special education establishment, it brought with it an understanding and requirement that public schools had a legal obligation to educate students with handicapping conditions. As this major upheaval was impacting public education, major upheavals were about to hit Maplebrook. In 1977 Dr. Moore reported the resignation of trustee Arthur White, Chair of the Education Committee. He went on to point out that the turnover of faculty and staff in the middle of their contracts has a negative impact on students. He asked the administration to examine the issues including the professional separation between faculty and house parents. During all this, Mrs. Rosalie Hurst, Chair of the Executive Committee announced the resignation of Lonnie L. Adams. Dr. Moore recommended the Trustees "Accept the resignation of Headmaster Lonnie L. Adams effective June 24, 1978.....with deep regret, but with the best of wishes. Mr. Adam's impact on Maplebrook has been profound and his service unmatched. As successor to Marge Finger, Lon Adams had been the "face" of Maplebrook and had made a positive impact on the Maplebrook family. His hard work and devotion to the growth of Maplebrook earned him the title "Mr. Maplebrook". The Executive Committee, chaired by Rosalie Hurst, recommended that Dick Howes, Business Manager and Dean Stickles, Principal share the responsibility for guiding Maplebrook School.

Several months later, the Executive Committee decided one head of school was best and asked Mr. Dick Howes to be interim Headmaster for one year as a search be conducted for a new headmaster. It was also during this time that Maplebrook became an approved school which enabled it to be eligible for funding. This meant that some parents could have some or all of the tuition paid by New York State. Mr. Dick Howes, in his role as acting headmaster, was authorized to contact Lonnie Adams and offer him the position of Headmaster – Principal as of July 1, 1979. During this period of uncertainty, there were a variety of staff changes and considerable faculty turnover. It was felt that a strong individual as the headmaster might bring back the stability of prior years. It seemed to be a period of uncertainty and confusion regarding the effects of PL94-142 on the funding issue in New York State as pertaining to Maplebrook School. It appears that New York State was requiring Maplebrook to change its admission policy in order remain a state funded school. Maplebrook refused and a representative from New York State visited the school. This person came to the conclusion that the students did not meet the criteria to apply for funding because they were not severely handicapped enough but, if Maplebrook changed the type of student they admitted, they would be placed on the approved funding list. The trustees indicated, "if we follow the States dictates, we would not be Maplebrook but would be a custodial type of school. And they agreed to maintain Maplebrook's traditional admission criteria and decline New York State funding. At a special meeting held on October 3, 1979, Don Warner, Chair of the Long Range Planning committee, stated, "Hence we trustees have a duty to look ahead now and plan for the moment and thereafter we must face the possibility, even probability, of no more state aid. Then do we knuckle under and go custodial – do we sharply raise tuition – do we reduce our size and retrench – or do we close down?" Were questions to be considered. As Maplebrook was wrestling with these issues, Marge Finger informed the board that she was planning for her retirement and is looking to relocate to Vermont to be closer to family after thirty-five years of dedication and service to Maplebrook School.

Marge Finger had been the heart and soul of Maplebrook School since its founding in 1945. This hard-working, dedicated woman shaped the customs and traditions while the school was in its infancy. Not surprisingly, many of these traditions have been continued to this day. Her warmth, kindness and concern touched many lives during her thirty-five years at Maplebrook. This diminutive woman with no formal training in special education and no business or administration experience in education went on to create the basis for one of the premiere special needs boarding schools of the 21st century. She had the support of a very committed board of trustees led by John Grant and of her two partners in founding Maplebrook – Coral "Sunny" Barlow and Serena Merck. During her final years at Maplebrook, she successfully passed on to her successor, Lonnie Adams, the importance of the Maplebrook "feel" which comes from being a small, student-centered school filled with warmth and individuals truly caring about the students they serve. Although staff are no longer "aunt" and "uncle" they continue to give the feeling of family. That is a major part of Aunt Marge's legacy.

The next few years witnessed more turbulence, uncertainty and turn-over. Dr. Gudarnatch, School physician since the 1950s, decided to retire and Dick Howes, who had been connected to Maplebrook as a parent, board member, interim Headmaster, Business Manager and supporter since 1961, also retired. Other key employees followed and the Headmaster's Report to the Board in May of 1983 indicated, "This has been a year of turmoil, anxiety and uncertainty. We began the year with a greatly decreased enrollment and the uncertainty as to our future was much on everyone's mind. Several key employees have departed and this has created a sense of desperation, at times, in those remaining as to who was next, who am I answerable to, etc. A most significant person in the lives of the student and headmaster left under most trying circumstances and this was catastrophic to the campus." In spite of all these setbacks, the School pushed forward under the leadership of Dr. Moore and the Board of Trustees. Mr. Adams indicated a new girls' dormitory was needed if we expected to attract female students. Mrs. Babcock suggested we start a fundraising campaign and she was willing to work with the headmaster on this effort. In addition to fundraising, Mr. Adams was crafting an advertising campaign to attract more students and hire replacement faculty. In 1984 Mr. Adams alerted the board to a "fantastic project undertaken by Mrs. Babcock who then informed the Board of Trustees of an art show to be given to benefit the school." This fundraiser was the foundation of Maplebrook's development efforts. Although initiated to support the equestrian program, it became the beginning of efforts to raising money through means other than tuition. Also Mr. and Mrs. Whitney Evans donated $50,000 to establish the Whitney Evans Professional Staff Development Fund. It was at this meeting that Lonnie Adams, Jerry Rossman and John Segalla suggested forming a committee to plan for the construction of a new dormitory for the girls. Now that the advertising campaign seemed to stabilize enrollments and the fundraising campaign put us in a position to be able to finance a new dormitory, Maplebrook was beginning to move forward in the areas of finance and admissions. Staff turnover, faculty housing, education, quality and clarity of mission were areas that needed attention. In an effort to promote stability and support, the headmaster and the trustees approved the hiring of Allan Gordon as Assistant to the Headmaster and William Smyth as Business Manager. Mr. Smyth worked closely with Mr. Adams to increase staff benefits by establishing a retirement program, unlimited sick time for all faculty and staff and increasing professional staff development opportunities. Mr. Gordon hired a curriculum coordinator to help develop social skills development and a more meaningful vocational component. Individual Education Plans were developed for each student.

It was in May 1985 that the board was informed of the death of Mrs. Serena Merck, one of the three co-founders of Maplebrook School. The Merck family had supported Maplebrook with many financial gifts since 1945.

Palm Beach Post – February 16, 1985

SERENA STEVENS MERCK Age 86. Of South Beach Rd.,Hobe Sound, died Thursday evening at her residence. Mrs. Merck was the daughter of the late George C. Stevens and Jose-prune S. Stevens. She was the widow of George W. Merck. Pres. Of Merck Chemical Co. Active in many philanthropies, and particularly concerned with the problem of Retardation in Children, Mrs. Merck received a number of Honors including an Honorary Doctor of Law (1981) from Fairfield University and membership in the Knights of Malta. During the First World War, she serves as a volunteer Nurse in New York City. When not in Florida, she made her home in Greenwich, Conn. And Rupert, VT. She is survived by a son, John H C Merck, Fairfield, CT; 2 daughters, Judith M. Buechner of Rupert, VT, and Serena Hatch of Beverly Farms, MA; one stepson, Albert W. Merck, Mendham NJ; seven grandchildren, one great granddaughter and one sister, Mrs. Donald White, of Old Greenwich, CT.

The Board of Trustees was acquiring new members committed to helping Maplebrook grow and prosper. In 1985 Mr. Mark Metzger joined the board and was followed by Mrs. Olivia Farr, the granddaughter of Mrs. Merck in 1986. Also in 1986 Maplebrook affiliated with Dutchess Community College to help administer the transitional vocational program established that year by Mr. Adams. The school was expanding its services to an older group of students to answer parents' need for finding programs for their students after they graduated from Maplebrook. In order to boast it's programming for vocational students, Maplebrook acquired a pizza restaurant near the school. This was accomplished with a gift from the Hatch family given in memory of Serena Merck.

In May 1987 the Personnel Committee of the Board sought to improve salaries of the staff to guarantee survival of Maplebrook. They also considered staff housing and staff attitude to try to ascertain reasons for high faculty/staff turnover. Other concerns such as fundraising, New York State Association of Independent Schools accreditation, board involvement and recruiting students were highlighted at that meeting. Later that year at the September board meeting, Dr. Moore stepped aside as Board President and Jerry Rossman was elected President of the board. Also Lonnie Adams made it known that he wished to retire. Mrs. Olivia Farr indicated The Merck Trust was willing to underwrite our fundraising efforts by retaining Eugene Dea and his staff to guide our efforts. Mr. Rossman, President of the board, announced, "it has been accepted by the Board that Dr. Roger Fazzone will be our new headmaster effective July 1, 1988 and we have accepted Mr. Adams' resignation with regret." Dr. Roger Fazzone was elected to the Board at this meeting and immediately started working with Jerry Rossman, Chair of the Executive Committee, on ways to help Maplebrook "right the ship".

Chapter 3

---ᔆᔆ---

Roger "Doc" Fazzone, Donna Konkolics And The Modern Era

Dr. Fazzone, a certified school psychologist, was the Dean at Dutchess Community College before he accepted the headmaster position at Maplebrook. A former professor at the college, Dr. Fazzone possessed nearly a decade of executive experience, plus he had been associated with Maplebrook first as an employee and later as a trustee since 1979. He had worked closely with Lon Adams for six months before becoming headmaster. Change was still in the air as Dr. Moore resigned after sixteen years of service on the Board of Trustees. Dr. Moore brought a dignity and air of professionalism to the board. He continued to be a friend of the school until his death in 2012.

From the Millerton News

Sharon – Roger Warren Moore died at his home in Sharon on June 26, 2012, with his family at his side. He was 95.

Born and raised in Stafford Springs, Conn, Roger graduated from Westminster School and matriculated at Williams College in 1935. Throughout high school and college he competed in track and field at a high level and was captain of the track team. He excelled in the high hurdles and was considered an Olympic-caliber athlete in that event.

After graduating from Williams in 1939 he pursued his medical degree at New York University, during which time he was introduced by a mutual friend to Jean Kissock of Forest Hills, NY and Laurelton, NJ. The couple married in 1943 and enjoyed a remarkable 61 years of marriage until Jean died in 2004.

During World War II he served as captain in the US Army Medical Corps, joining the military in 1944 and receiving an honorable discharged in 1946. His service included 20 months overseas. He was awarded the European African Middle Eastern Ribbon and the World War II Victory Ribbon.

He did his medical residency at the VA Hospital in Van Nuys, Calif., where the couple's first two children were born. The family moved east in 1953 and settled in Sharon where their third child was born. There Dr. Moore joined Sharon Clinic founders Drs. Fisher, Fowler, Gevalt and Noble, becoming one of eight physicians considered to be the original core of the successful medical group.

Dr. Moore's generosity and tireless dedication to patients made him one of the Northwest Corner's most popular and respected internists. He would often leave his residence in the middle of the night to attend to patients, and routinely made house calls at a time when that tradition was fading. He was known not to charge those who were unable to afford medical care. On Christmas morning, hospital rounds had to be completed first, while at home the family would wait to begin the day until he returned. Dr. Moore was an attending physician at Sharon Hospital and sat on the hospital board for many years.

After the Sharon Clinic closed he maintained his private practice in the building with a core staff that for a time included his daughter Sharon. While he officially retired in 1996 at the age of 80 after more than a50 years of service, he remained very much a caregiver and medical advisor to those in need, and made regular visits to both Sharon Hospital and Noble Horizons.

Dr. Moore was deeply involved with Maplebrook School in Amenia, NY, and in 1997 received the Headmaster's Award for his volunteer service as a trustee (1965-1988) and president of the Board of Trustees (1973 – 1987).

At various times he served as president of the Sharon Historical Society and president of the Sharon Fish and Game Club.

As an experienced sailor, Roger loved being on the water. He was a member of the U.S. Power Squadron and was skilled at small boat handling as well as celestial navigation. From the mid- to late- 1960's the family would explore the New England Coast while living for a week on chartered 30- and 40- foot sloops or schooners captained by Dr. Moore. In the summer of 1974, at age 57, he completed an Atlantic Crossing with three other sailors. The four men sailed the 45-foot yawl Perelandra from Halifax, Nova Scotia to Bantry Bay, Ireland, covering 2,309 miles in 16 days. Propelled by gale-force winds, they arrived three days ahead of schedule.

He was a naturally gifted musician with a fine voice who sang in the church choir and occasionally played piano for family and friends. A long time jazz enthusiast, he especially loved the big band and swing eras and listed Oscar Peterson as one of his favorite pianists.

The main issues plaguing the school at this time remain faculty/staff turnover, enrollments and fundraising. Unfortunately, Eugene Dea, the fundraising consultant hired by the school died of a heart attack in November 1988. The challenges facing the new headmaster and the board of trustees were the long standing issues of staff turnover, declining enrollments, fundraising, NYSAIS accreditation and clarity of the mission and goals of the school.

Dr. Fazzone, because of his working at Maplebrook part-time as a school psychologist and his background in college administration, was aware of some of the major issues Maplebrook School needed to address. The most important issue was enrollments. Maplebrook needed to examine why enrollments were declining and develop a plan to remedy the situation. The second major issue was faculty/staff/board turnover. Throughout its history, Maplebrook had faced a significant turnover rate. That situation had to be remedied if Maplebrook was to become a school of excellence. The third area of concern was a deteriorating physical plant with old wooden barn-like buildings in poor condition that greeted prospective parents and/or teachers when they first visited the school. Finally, there needed to be something distinctive about the Maplebrook educational experience that would assist students in realizing their objectives.

Enrollments: during his time as a school psychologist, Dr. Fazzone observed many students graduating with an eighth grade diploma and going on to Riverview or another private high school in order to earn their high school diploma. His plan was to have Maplebrook apply to become a New York registered high school and then develop the vocational/transitional program into a program of many postsecondary options. The year 1988 was a significant one for Maplebrook School because of the changes brought about the new administration and the responses to external forces all schools must make. Dr. Fazzone appointed Lori Hale as the Admissions Director in 1988. Mrs. Hale, a speech therapist, had been at Maplebrook since 1982 and would hold a variety of key positions over the next quarter century at Maplebrook. The academic program was lacking substance and structure and Miss Donna Konkolics, a colleague from Dutchess Community College was hired as principal in 1989. She was to begin to shape the process of creating a high school level academic program. Mr. James Walsh was to initiate the process of having Maplebrook become a registered high school and was hired in 1989 as Director of Career Programs. Mr. Donald Capalbo, a houseparent, was hired as Director of Student Activities and was instrumental in the growth of programing in the dormitories and the sports program. While these activities were taking place, the boys' dormitory and Windridge were remodeled and the Annex was converted into three apartments to start our apartment living program. The Little Professors Day Care Center got its start in 1989 with Susan Anderson as the first director. The Eagles Nest (school store) was founded that same year under the direction of Donald Capalbo. Mr. Rossman hosted several meetings in his offices in New York City to discuss retaining the company of the late Eugene Dea to teach Maplebrook how to conduct an annual fund campaign and to learn the basics of conducting a capital campaign. Dr. Fazzone hired Aaron Donsky for three months to help Maplebrook acquire 25 IBM computers to use in the academic program.

With all the positive changes taking place at the school there were still issues needing to be resolved. Mark Metzger, Chairman of the Finance Committee reported to the trustees at the March 2, 1989 meeting that the restaurant was losing money even after a change in management. Dr. Fazzone reported that he attended several NYSAIS meetings in preparation for the accreditation visit by the visiting team in March 1990. Also Dr. Fazzone developed a maintenance plan "to insure the physical plant receives the attention necessary to maintain and/or exceed all state standards and parent expectations. The repair to all buildings and paving of all roadways will be scheduled and Maplebrook will have an excellent looking campus again." He also reported the hiring of Mr. Joe Staggers, Maplebrook's first development officer.

In March 1990, Maplebrook hosted six interns from a social pedagog college in Sweden. This was an effort to become more international and later that year the school would host its first Japanese intern. Dr. Fazzone also brought an academic governance model to Maplebrook where faculty committees have input to the governance of the school. He formed the Curriculum, Professional Staff Development, Buildings and Grounds, Admission/Graduation committees and filled them with faculty. The NYSAIS visiting team made their accreditation visit on April 1, 1990 and reported "Maplebrook as a school in great transition and they like transition. The visiting team will come back in two years to see if we have done what we stated we do." The capital campaign fundraising effort was at a standstill and Maplebrook hired Kathy Gallo to become our second development officer. Dr. Fazzone developed the Responsibility Increases Self Esteem Program that year and all faculty and staff were trained in its purpose and procedures. Enrollments were slowly climbing and total students at the school exceeded sixty for the first time with the bulk of the increase coming from the career program.

In the midst of all the activity surrounding new programs, preparations for the accreditation visit, new staffing, a re-emphasis on academics, high school registration and repair of campus facilities, Dr. Fazzone and Mr. Rossman found time to expand upon their already good relationship to form a close and enduring friendship. Jerry would travel with Roger to the annual NAPSEC Conferences in Florida where they would attend training sessions together on such topics as board management, fundraising and personnel issues. They became well known to the NAPSEC Board of Directors and Jerry Rossman became knowledgeable of other NAPSEC member schools. They also attended conferences and training workshops in California to obtain further training in fundraising techniques from leaders like Jerry Panas, in the development community. They also met with donors regarding Maplebrook's first capital campaign.

The partnership between Jerry Rossman and Roger Fazzone started when Roger accepted the position of headmaster in 1988. As he stated in the prologue to a booklet entitled "*The Partnership years*",

It's with warmth and comfort that I recall my first day at Maplebrook School campus back in 1979, and I have to admit to feeling the same way almost 30 years later. Each day, getting up and going to work is a pleasure.

I began my Maplebrook career as the school's part-time psychologist. At the same time I was a professor of child studies at a local community college. For about 20 hours each week at Maplebrook, I conducted counseling groups, administered psychological tests and advised faculty and staff on students' behavioral issues. These experiences were therapeutic for me as well. At the College, I gave courses in developing programs for residential centers whose children were in need of greater supervision. It was interesting to teach these courses during the morning and observe students at Maplebrook each afternoon and evening, a unique opportunity to witness both the theory and its practice.

By 1983 I became a full-time administrator at the college and was no longer available to work at Maplebrook. Prior to this, I had been invited to become a member of the Maplebrook Board, and I was happy to be able to remain on the Board.

As an administrator at the college, I learned the importance of board/chair relationships in educational administration. I received an important lesson when the unionized faculty there attempted to oust a reforming president. Fortunately, the board's chairman had both judicious intelligence and strong moral character, and the college president survived.

Thus, when I was asked to consider the position of Headmaster at Maplebrook School, my first thoughts were about the stability of the Board of Trustees. I had been on the Board since 1982 and felt I knew each

member very well. The chairman was Jerome I. Rossman, Jr. (Jerry) who impressed me as an enthusiastic and dedicated individual. I had also learned that a healthy partnership between the headmaster and board was based on mutual respect and frequent communication.

After chatting with Jerry and Lon Adams, the outgoing headmaster, over a very long lunch, Jerry and I felt we could work together and Jerry submitted my name to the trustees in December 1987. As headmaster, my responsibility would be to listen to the ideas and suggestions of various constituencies at the school and bring significant ones to Jerry's attention. My college experience had taught me that it is the responsibility of both the board chairman and headmaster to keep the board well informed and on task.

Jerry recognized immediately that the headmaster was charged with the day-to-day management of the school and should be trusted to do so. I would not report to individual trustees, but to the board as a whole. We had a mutual desire to make Maplebrook the best school of its kind in the country. Our partnership was responsible for much of the advancement made at Maplebrook since 1988.

While expanding Maplebrook's national and international presence, activity continued on the campus. Maplebrook students were more heavily involved in team sports as the schedule grew to involve schools such as Kildonan, Hotchkiss and Sherman School under the careful leadership of Donald Capalbo. The games attracted good sized crowds made up of teachers, parents, students and others including Board Members and alumni. The Howes family attended many games with Dick, Betty and Rick cheering the Eagles to a good number of victories. Donald Capalbo also initiated the Maplebrook enrichment program that featured more than twenty eight activities that students could join and enjoy in the evenings or on weekends. He also started a school store, The Eagles Nest, to support the teen canteen recreation center. His work reflected the enthusiasm that permeated all that worked at Maplebrook during the last decade of the twentieth century. In 1989, the Little Professors Day Care Center was established on the Maplebrook Campus to serve Maplebrook employees with young children as well as the Amenia community. The quality daycare facility was also established to train students from the Center for Advancement of Postsecondary Studies (CAPS) to be day care workers and was modeled after the program offered at Dutchess Community College. Susan Anderson (Miss Susan) was appointed the first Director and under her leadership the day care center experienced substantial growth as well as significant acceptance by the local community. The CAPS students received outstanding training from Miss Susan. The Day Care Center was housed in Sollar Hall until growing enrollments necessitated a move to what is now the TLC campus.

The Little Professors Day Care Center received recognition from Dutchess County Child Development Council and was approved by the Dutchess County Health Department. In addition, it was a recognized training site for several colleges who trained day care workers.

The Boys dormitory, Evans Hall, was completely remodeled with new windows, new lighting, and new furniture in 1991. This needed to be accomplished because of the new girl's dormitory built in 1986 created a level of dissatisfaction with the parents of boys who were living in a dark, crowded dormitory. Once renovated, the boy's dormitory was expanded to add several new rooms.

Enrollments in the CAPS program were rapidly growing and required a plan to relocate the living quarters to the west campus where the old administration building was taken down and a new dormitory for girls was constructed with the help of a large gift from the Wilson Family. Just across the lawn the Annex building was totally renovated into three apartments capable of housing up to ten students enrolled in the Apartment Living Program which prepared students for the rigors of managing their own apartments. With a generous gift from David Weinstein, The Sky's The Limit Apartment complex opened in 1990. Finally, the Headmasters House was converted into a dormitory for 10 boys with attached apartments for faculty with dormitory responsibilities. The West campus was named the C.A.P.S. Campus and continued the philosophy of John Finger who toiled for many years teaching students work skills on the same ground where Maplebrook School started.

In 1997, Dr. Fazzone appointed Miss Doreen Bianchi head of the Maplebrook Teachers Institute. The purpose of the Institute was to create a training program for teachers modelled after the Maplebrook faculty methodologies which included multi-sensory instruction, individualized tutoring and principles of the RISE program. The latter was supported by a grant from the Shelby-Cullum Davis Foundation and enabled training sessions to take place in New York, Connecticut, Florida, Arizona and California thus bringing the Maplebrook name and reputation to professionals nationwide. Maplebrook sponsored an International Symposium on its campus in Amenia bringing in speakers such as Ulla Schroder from the Socialpedagog College of Stockholm, Sweden, Mary Gale Budsisz of the Council of Children with Behavior Disorders, Mr. Frank Mulhern of the Anderson Center for Autistic Children and Professor Robby Luddy from Buena Vista University in Iowa. The symposium attracted teachers from many different states as far away as Oregon and Washington.

Later that year, the Samara Foundation was established as a vehicle to award scholarships to enrolling students. The Samara Foundation was founded by Arnold and Seima Sollar in 1986. The Sollar's son, David, was enrolled as a student at Maplebrook for several years and they wished to assist Lonnie Adams, the Headmaster, in raising monies for capital improvements needed by the school. They became friendly with an entrepreneur from nearby Lakeville who had "connections" with the popular singer, John Denver. They suggested to the Sollars that John Denver might be persuaded to perform a benefit concert for Maplebrook at Lime Rock Park in nearby Lakeville, CT. Arnold Sollar, being an attorney thought it wise to establish a not for profit foundation to sponsor the event thus avoiding any liability for Maplebrook in such an undertaking.

After months of discussion and planning, the promotor of the concert indicated she was unable to secure the date and the venue and the concert never happened, leaving the Samara Foundation dormant for almost ten years. Then in 1995, Arnold Sollar approached Dr. Fazzone to ask if Maplebrook would like to have a legally constituted foundation. Years later the name was changed to the Maplebrook School Foundation.

Also in the mid 1990s the Board of Trustees formed committee 2,000 headed by Olivia Farr, the granddaughter of George and Serena Merck. The Committee 2,000 was constituted in order to do fundraising to build a new gymnasium and develop long range plans for future Maplebrook improvements. They convened every month or so in New York City alternating between Jerry Rossman's office in midtown and The Wall Street Offices of Dempsey and William's brokerage. Olivia Farr was a bright, articulate young woman who brought a wealth of ideas to the Board of Trustees of Maplebrook School. The Committee 2,000, under her leadership took the lead in establishing a capital campaign for the building of Rossman Hall (gymnasium) and several scholarships. In addition, Committee 2,000 heightened our awareness of the concept of planned giving by forming the George and Serena Merck Legacy Society.

In 1996 Dr. Fazzone was elected President of the International Association of Special Education and Chairman of the 5th Biennial IASE Conference to be held in Capetown, South Africa. While there he trained several hundred teachers in the principles of the R.I.S.E. program. Keeping up its emphasis on international collaboration, Maplebrook sponsored a classical musical concert in Dutchess County, NY, featuring musicians from the Conservatory of Music in Tashkient, Uzbeckistan. On the national level, Maplebrook basketball team played a rival school in the Brendan Byrne Arena, the home of the New York Nets NBA team. All those activities helped Maplebrook School to be known in many states and internationally as well. Dr. Fazzone and Mr. Rossman carried the word regarding Maplebrook far and wide by attending NAPSEC, NAIS, and LDA Conferences in addition to attending fundraising training sessions in many states.

Maplebrook's computer capability consisted of ten apple computers donated by parents in the 1980s. Dr. Fazzone, a computer illiterate, sought help from Aaron Donskey, a professional colleague from Dutchess Community College, who procured a grant for 12 IBM Computers to be used in Maplebrook's classrooms and office. The old Apple computers were relocated to the dormitories. The faculty and staff received extensive training on their use. Dr. Donsky, an expert in long range planning, met with the Maplebrook Trustees to educate them regarding the importance of long range strategic planning. Jerry Rossman was very impressed with these conversations and through Olivia Farr, encouraged the Committee 2,000 to envision what was needed for Maplebrook to become the best school of its kind in the world.

Since its founding, Maplebrook has had the traditional Board-Headmaster style of governance where the Board of Trustees delegates responsibility to the Headmaster to administer the school within the policies established by the Trustees. When Dr. Fazzone was appointed Headmaster in 1988, he envisioned an Academic Governance model borrowed from higher education. The concept of academic governance in Postsecondary Institutions consists of a governing Board, the

President, a team of Administrators (deans), department chairs and some sort of student representation. To apply this model to a small school with a history of faculty/staff frequent turnover would be a challenge. During the 1980s and 1990s Maplebrook hired several key faculty and staff that became the bedrock of stability for the school. Donna Konkolics, Chair of the Child Care Program at a local college was hired as Maplebrook's Dean of Academics. She provided a sense of leadership and energy to a school entrenched in methods and procedures that were less than productive. Lori Hale, Speech Therapist, filled the position of Principal on a temporary basis before being shifted to Admission Director where she facilitated the school's highest enrollments to date. Years later, she became the Director of the Center for Advancement of Postsecondary Studies (CAPS) where she brought leadership and stability.

In 1993, Ms. Jennifer Scully was hired as a part time daycare worker and part time faculty with dormitory responsibilities. She became an excellent teacher, an outstanding coach bringing Maplebrook its only undefeated season for its field hockey team. She later became Director of Enrollment Management Services (Admissions) and Transition planning before becoming the Assistant Head of School for Postsecondary Studies and Director of the Institute of Collegiate and Career Studies.

Also in 1994, Maplebrook School hired Mr. John Tomasetti as a faculty member with dormitory responsibilities. John and his family lived in the boy's dormitory and later became the first supervisors at the Melbrooke campus before becoming the Director of Experiential Learning on the Postsecondary Campus.

The Center for Experiential Learning was established in 1995 to develop some structure and pedagogy for our internship program. This program allowed students to be placed in a community worksite for a half a day five days per week. The experiential learning model starts with the student having a concrete work experience then he/she reflects on that experience and then he/she analyzes what he/she did while working and then the student uses the new ideas gained from the experience. This type of learning is an ideal multisensory way for youngsters with learning issues to master different concepts. This model became the heart and soul of the methodology utilized in Maplebrook's postsecondary programs. Also in the early 1990's, Mr. Ken Hale was appointed Business Manager, a position he holds to this day. Ken Hale has brought a steady hand and vigilant eye to every stage of the amazing growth experienced by Maplebrook during the past quarter century. In addition, many faculty hired at this time, remained for long periods of time. Finally, Mr. Joe Selino and Mr. Gary Ackerman, Heads of Maintenance for the High School and Postsecondary campuses came to Maplebrook during this time period and remain part of the leadership of Maplebrook.

The academic governance model, which relies on faculty/staff sharing responsibility to shape Maplebrook's, continued growth through committee work, which may have been part of the reason why the constant turnover of key staff finally ended at Maplebrook. Faculty/ Staff involvement in committees, such as curriculum, professional staff development, and facilities and safety helped individuals feel part of the continued progress of the school. They and others had the opportunity to be part of the long range planning committee, the accreditation committee and several ad hoc committees that were formed over the years.

The Board of Trustees had been a supportive group since the founding of the school, but it had been marked by a good amount of instability due to the changing membership. Parents who were Board Members tended to leave the Board when their child graduated the School. The exceptions were Dick Howes and Jerry Rossman. A review of the official Board records shows that all other parent Board members resigned from the Board within three years of their child's graduation. In 1995, George T. Whalen, Jr. from Millbrook was elected to the Board of Trustees. George was a semi- retired real estate broker who also conducted an insurance business and owned the Bank of Millbrook. He believed a strong Board of Trustees worked through its various committees who would report their deliberations at the Board Meeting. He served on Boards of private school in the past and realized that parents who were trustees were often conflicted by what is important to the school. Knowing this, he favored using local business men and women to constitute school boards. In order to have parental representation on the Board, he suggested utilizing parents who had children, who had already graduated from the school.

George had a fondness for the school because, as he likes to point out, "my wife Ann was born and raised in Amenia just a few hundred yards from the main entrance to the school." Over the years, George helped attract many prominent Dutchess County business leaders to the Maplebrook Board including the County Executive, William "Bill" Steinhaus and reknowned businessman Emil Panichi. George became friendly with Dr. Fazzone and over the next twenty years became an important member of the Board who played a key role in shaping Maplebrook's future.

The mid 1990s brought with it a flurry of activity and innovation. After converting the Headmaster's home into the CAPS boy's dormitory Maplebrook bought 11 acres of land and a 100 year old house from the Twigg Family. This land which adjoined the CAPS campus became the Headmaster's Home and was renamed Mill Pond. The old bike barn on the main campus was completely renovated and became the student center and was named after David Brachfeld, a student who died while on summer vacation. David was a terrific young man who made tremendous progress during his three years at Maplebrook. Unfortunately, that was not the only death the school experienced, a year later the school was rocked by the death of Clayton Feig, another student who died while on summer vacation. Shortly after, a third student, Ann Marie Zawatsky also died while home on vacation. These deaths moved the faculty and students and counseling protocols were established to assist faculty and students in dealing with grief.

Maplebrooks fiftieth anniversary was celebrated at the newly constructed Segalla's Golf Course. John Segalla, a local businessman, a former Maplebrook Trustee, was fond of the school and was very friendly with Dr. Fazzone. His vocal support of the school helped "town-grown" relationships and he was instrumental in the school forming a connection between Dr. Fazzone and Town Supervisor, Ralph Vinchiarello. This connection fostered several mutual projects between Maplebrook and the Town of Amenia.

Around the same time, three parents formed a partnership to buy a large bed and breakfast close to the center of town known as The Palmer House. They renovated the entire structure into four apartments and built another structure with four more apartments with the goal of filling each apartment with a Maplebrook graduate who would work in Amenia. They renamed The Palmer House, Melbrooke. They added several other families as partners within the first year and they renovated an old barn which they rented to Maplebrook for the new home of the Maplebrook Day Care Center and Preschool. They also constructed a hydroponics tomato farm that produced more than 1,000 pounds of tomatoes per week. All their children were trained to work in the tomato farm. Maplebrook was contracted to supervise their living arrangements. The parents were very involved with the remodeling and greenhouse work. The original three students were quite compatible but as additional residents were added and compromises occurred, differences became apparent. For several years, during the late 1990s Melbrooke was a model of innovation and success.

With the new gymnasium (Rossman Hall) completed and in full use, the old gym was renovated and became home to the Clayton Feig Theater in 1997, in addition a library and computer room were constructed in part of the old gym. Also, a new soccer field and track were constructed on the lower field of the main campus and the upper field became home to two tennis courts gifted by the Rossman Family.

As Maplebrook approached its 55th year as a school, it's campus had been transformed into an elite boarding school with playing fields, a library, a theater, attractive dormitories ad a seasoned faculty supported by a stable Board of Trustees. Dr. Fazzone and Mr. Rossman carried the Maplebrook message across the United States and under the guidance of Lori Hale, the Maplebrook enrollments reached 104 full time equivalents students compromised of 102 boarders and 4 day students, the largest enrollment in its first fifty five years of existence. Because many of these enrollments were postsecondary students enrolling in the CAPS program, further expansion of the West Campus was necessary and construction was started on two modular duplexes for faculty and one for students. The horse barn was renovated and turned into the CAPS student center and renamed the Babcock-Cloney Student Union. In 1999, George Whalen and Roger Fazzone negotiated the purchase of 40 acres of land from Ann Linden. This land bordered the main campus and allowed Maplebrook to expand its playing fields to accommodate the growing number of team sports.

Once again, the Headmaster's Home (Millpond) was being converted to be used for student space and a small house on Mygatt Road was purchased for the replacement Headmaster's residence. As Maplebrook approached its 55th year, as a school, the growth of the school began to stretch the responsibilities of the Headmaster where he had to spend more and more time off campus tending to business in the town and in the county. After months of discussion with the Board of Trustees, a new administrative structure was developed where Dr. Fazzone would become President and be responsible for all external issues such as enrollments, fundraising, and the growth of the school while Miss Konkolics would take over as Head of School and be responsible for the everyday running of the school. They would share responsibility of articulating with the Board of Trustees.

In the fifty-five years since its founding, Maplebrook had grown from 8 students in three buildings on seven acres of land with 10 faculty and staff to 109 students in 22 buildings on 121 acres with seventy full time and part time faculty and staff. All of this was possible by strong enrollments in the High School and CAPS programs, a stable faculty and staff, a very supportive Board of Trustees and innovative and visionary executive leadership.

As the new millennium approached, Maplebrook continued to grow and prosper. It became even more involved in the local community with Dr. Fazzone being elected President of the Amenia Historical Society and was a founding Board Member of the Indian Rock One Room Schoolhouse Association. He and Mr. Rossman continued their national outreach at various conferences and workshops. With enrollments growing in the High School, the Board realized a new classroom building was necessary. The administration proposed a new building, Babcock Hall, be built parallel to Ferkauf Hall as phase one of the project. When that was completed, the venerable old schoolhouse was ceremoniously razed and a new modern schoolhouse called Thalheimer Hall replaced it. The building projects completed the $3.5 million Rainbow campaign started in 2001 after Dr. Fazzone and Mr. Rossman attended a workshop in California by famed fundraiser Jerry Panas. The workshop was entitled "How to design a Capital Campaign". Part of the Rainbow Campaign was the remodeling of the old farmhouse on the main campus and naming it Howes Hall after Richard "Dick" Howes who passed a few years earlier.

In May of 2001 Dr. Fazzone, Mr. Wilson and Mr. Whalen became the nominating committee and continued to appoint quality individuals to the Board of Trustees. On September 11, 2001 the World Trade Center in New York City was struck by Terrorists and the world around Maplebrook changed forever. Later that year, Maplebrook was reaccredited by the New York Association of Independent Schools (NYSAIS) and the Middle States Association of Colleges and Schools. Shortly thereafter, the peace court near Babcock Hall was dedicated to all who perished in that event.

In 2004 the experiment known as Melbrooke Farm began to unravel. Student incompatibility began to show and the parents who owned and operated the farm began to experience discord. The collaboration became too tense and they dissolved the agreement and offered to sell the land and buildings to Maplebrook. Once again, George Whalen and Roger Fazzone, acting on behalf of the Board, negotiated a purchase of 10 acres and all the buildings for the school. Melbrooke would become the Transition Living Center for eight (8) C.A.P.S. seniors.

In 2005, the $3.5 million Rainbow Campaign was completed. The small school, established by three women with the dream of establishing a school for youngsters who learned differently, had raised $3.5 million to solidify its place as a premier boarding school for students with learning challenges. Later that year, one of the last of the "Aunts" and "Uncles" passed away. You will recall that earlier in Maplebrook history, Marge Finger initiated key staff being referred to as Aunt Marge or Uncle John, etc. In 2005 one of the truly beloved "aunts" passed away. Ruth Bodner had come to work at Maplebrook when Lonnie Adams was Headmaster. She was a loving motherly woman who treated each student as he/she was her own child. Appreciated and admired by many alumni and parents, Aunt Ruth remained with the school as Alumni liaison when Lonnie Adams retired in 1988. She corresponded with many graduates by letter and telephone since this was before email and the internet. Ruth also attended Alumni reunions as long as her heath allowed. She was truly a remarkable person who cared for and loved the students and alumni of Maplebrook School. A true Maplebrook School legend, the main wing of the Evans Hall was dedicated in her name shortly after her death. That same year, the girls dormitory was renamed Marjorie Finger Hall after the woman who meant so much to the early years of the school. A few years later, the school subdivided the TLC property into two 5 acre parcels, one parcel contained all the buildings and the second parcel contained the greenhouse. George Whalen and Roger Fazzone negotiated the sale of the second parcel to the fire department of the town of Amenia.

Later that year, the Chapel was built and dedicated to Johnny Merck, Maplebrook's first student. The chapel was located in a prominent place on campus so that it was the first building seen by anyone driving on campus; a fitting tribute to the Schools first student and the Merck Family.

In 2006 The Samara Foundation appointed its Board of Directors separate from Maplebrook Trustees. Dr. Fazzone, Mr. Rossman and Mr. Whalen recruited a dedicated group of individuals who would help guide the Samara Foundation to new heights of success on behalf of Maplebrook School and the Amenia Community.

The Samara foundation was renamed the Maplebrook School Foundation and appointed Mrs. Lori Hale as the first Executive Director. Lori Hale came to Maplebrook as a speech therapist in 1983 when Lon Adams was Headmaster. She remained at Maplebrook when Dr. Fazzone became Headmaster and she held a variety of positions while working with Dr. Fazzone. She was appointed Acting Principal in 1989 and then returned to admissions work when Donna Konkolics was appointed Dean of Academics and Principal. Lori then dedicated herself to increasing the Maplebrook enrollment to a record 117 students in 2003 when she took the position of Director of The Center for Advancement of Postsecondary Studies. Mrs. Hale understood the culture of Maplebrook School and was the ideal choice to develop the growth of the Maplebrook Foundation and become the "face" of Maplebrook in the local community. During her career at Maplebrook, Lori learned the intricacies of a growing boarding school by "wearing many hats". Not only was this Lori's one and only job after completing her Bachelor's degree but she married and raised three children while living and working at the school. She has been the epitome of living the boarding school dream. After her children grew older Lori became even more involved in the local community. She was on the Indian Mountain School Board of Trustees and the President of the Amenia Lions Club. In her role as Executive Director of the Maplebrook School Foundation she perfected many fundraising special events such as the Bowling Tournament held each February, the Golf Tournament held each June, The Classic Car show held during early September, The Annual walk/run over the Hudson held each spring to benefit the Panichi Center, the Kentucky Derby/Art show and sale held each May and the annual silent auction held on Parents Weekend every fall. There are many ad hoc special events of which Lori is also a part. In her spare time, Lori also conducts the Annual Fund Campaign.

As mentioned earlier, the year 2000 saw a major restructuring of the administration of Maplebrook School. The year 2000 brought with it predictions of disaster and calamity. Y2K as it was known. For months before the stroke of midnight on January 1, 2000, analysts speculated that entire computer networks would crash causing widespread calamities for the entire world that had grown dependent on computers. Those predictions of confusion and disaster did not occur. Nor did they occur at Maplebrook when Donna Konkolics took over as the Head of School from Roger Fazzone. Donna quietly administered the Academic Program and the entire school according to the precepts of

Boarding School Life developed at Maplebrook since the Marge Finger years.

Donna came to Maplebrook in 1983 as a part time counselling group facilitator. Her full time job was training college students to work effectively in a variety of residential settings. She was very active in the Association of Child Care Workers (ACCW) and was very familiar with all the private schools and residential centers in Dutchess County. She also helped develop the first after school centers in New York State and was instrumental in planning innovative programs for children.

In 2006 after twenty years as the Chairman of the Board of Trustees, Mr. Jerry Rossman decided to relinquish the chair responsibilities as he desired to move into retirement. He remained on the Board as a trustee and Mr. Mark Metzger, who had been a trustee since 1984, became the Chairman of the Board. Mark was recruited to the Board by Lonnie Adams and held a variety of positions on the Board including Chairman of the Finance Committee, Chairman of the Development Committee and Vice-Chairman of the Board. Mark is an attorney from the Poughkeepsie Area of Dutchess County and is widely known for being the consummate volunteer in addition to his long tenure at Maplebrook. Mr. Metzger has been involved with the Dutchess County ARC and the New York ARC for many years. His legal expertise helped guide Maplebrook during those years.

In 2007, while attending the National Learning Disabilities Conference in Chicago, Mr. Rossman and Dr. Fazzone were introduced to Dr. Kun Rhee, Vice President of Daegu University in South Korea. Jerry Rossman's jovial personality made Dr. Rhee feel relaxed and helped forge a bond between Dr. Rhee and Dr. Fazzone. They met several times during that conference and decided to establish a formal relationship between the two educational institutes. The following year, Dr. Rhee and several research colleagues from Daegu visited Maplebrook School and signed a formal agreement to cooperate with each other and establish an exchange program. Dr. Fazzone would visit Daegu later that year to complete the agreement. Also during 2008 Mr. Whalen and Dr. Fazzone were recruiting additional members for the Maplebrook School Foundation in preparation for the next capital campaign. It was at that time that the Foundation established the first of several non-need based scholarships. A year later the Northeast Collegiate Institute was established to assist those students who aspired for a true collegiate experience. In 2009, Woodcliff was renovated and two faculty apartments were added to help support Maplebrooks growing faculty. The administration reported the student enrollment was growing in the High School and C.A.P.S. program causing overcrowding in the dining hall. As these facts became known to the trustees and Directors along with the Whalen, Rossman and Fazzone Team started conversations regarding the next capital campaign.

The Level II dormitory on the C.A.P.S. campus was dedicated to Sunny Barlow, one of the three founders of Maplebrook School in May of 2010. Barlow Hall also housed some classroom space on the lowest of its three levels. Later that year Ron Wilson was appointed Associate Head of School in charge of Postsecondary programs.

Dr. Fazzone and Mr. Rossman continued to attend workshops on fundraising and capital campaigns conducted by renowned fundraiser Jerry Panas. In 2011, they scheduled him to conduct a workshop for staff, trustees and directors in order to prepare for the largest capital campaign in Maplebrook history. The Forging the Future comprehensive capital campaign was to build the Whalen Dining Hall and the Burnett Internet Café which would become the social hub of the campus and the Etkin Environmental Center, a certified wildlife habitat and sustainability center. In addition the construction of Hilfiger Hall would provide the venue for an emphasis on fine arts. Attached to Hilfiger Hall would be a performing arts center with rooms for music practice and vocal instruction. Talent shows and drama productions would also be featured in that building. Perhaps the centerpiece of the project would be a new natatorium featuring a saltwater pool and a refurbished wellness center. All this plus some additional scholarship money would take five years to complete, at a cost of more than $5 million. The original steering committee for the silent phase was Dr. Fazzone, Mr. Rossman and Mr. Whalen.

In September 2012, the high school became an iPad campus providing every student with a new iPad and the faculty received training in providing instruction on the iPads. Later that year, Howes Hall renovations were completed and the Founders reception room dedicated. The next year, Mr. Ron Wilson visited Daegu University as part of our exchange agreement and the bond between the two educational institutions grew stronger. Later that year, Lori Hale, Executive Director and Carrie Ducillo, Event Coordinator became the first employees of the Maplebrook School Foundation and the public phase of the Forging the Future capital campaign officially started. Later that year, The Maplebrook Classic Car Show was unveiled on the main campus. In June of 2016, Mr. Jerry Rossman retired to Florida due to failing health. The Trustees voted him Emeritus status because of his lifetime of assistance to the School.

In 2015 Dr. Fazzone and Donna Konkolics visited Jerry Rossman in Florida and later visited with Arnold Sollar who also lives in Florida. The purpose of the visit was to inform Mr. Sollar that Sollar Hall was in poor repair and would be taken down to make way for the Natatorium. They proposed to build a new Sollar Hall on the Institute Campus. Mr. Sollar graciously offered to help with the cost of the project. Later that year, Jerry Rossman passed away.

Jerome Rossman Obituary as published in the New York Times on Tuesday, April 11, 2017.

Jerome I. Rossman, Jr., 88 years old, formerly of Scarsdale and Purchase, New York, passed away peacefully at his home in Jupiter, Florida on Wednesday, July 8, 2015, surrounded by his family. Jerry proudly served his country in the U.S. Marine Corps. He was a truly kind man who had many significant friendships in all aspects of his life, and will be remembered dearly by all for his keen sense of humor, his loyalty and his love of family. Jerry dedicated his life to furthering education and independence for individuals who learn differently. He served as Chairman of the Board of the Maplebrook School in Amenia, NY which focuses on quality academic programs for youngsters with learning differences. Maplebrook provides individualized instruction, where students are assisted in reaching his/her academic, social, vocational and physical potential. Jerry and his wife, Eva, were deeply involved with Maplebrook and the Maplebrook "Parents Association" for many years, which their son Peter, attended. As Peter was graduating from Maplebrook, Jerry and two other Maplebrook parents founded the Chapel Haven, with the vision to establish an independent living facility in New Haven, CT providing lifelong individualized services for people with developmental and social disabilities, empowering them to live independent and self-determined lives. Jerry's devotion and determination paid off. Today, Chapel Haven is an award-winning, nationally accredited school and transitional program serving 250-plus adults with a variety of abilities and needs. Chapel Haven teaches independent living. Jerry is survived by his loving wife of over 60 years, Eva; his adoring children, Peter Rossman, Karen Fleck and Bryan Fleck, husband of Karen.

After seventy years of growth and promise Maplebrook had fulfilled the dreams of its founders and become one of the finest boarding schools for students who learn differently. Marge Finger, Serena Merck, and Sunny Barlow possessed a vision of a school that would provide the highest level of education for individuals with mild to moderate learning issues. They wanted those youngsters to have an educational experience that would prepare them for life and one in which they could be proud. Their dream has been fulfilled Maplebrook is the finest school of its kind in the world!

Appendix

Mason, Truth

Merck, Serena

Stevens, Margaret

Troutman, Warren

Weaver, William

<u>1960s</u>

Deister, Margaret

Finger, Marjorie

Grant, John

Howes, Richard

Hurst, Rosalie

Hyde, Katherine

Logan, H.A.

Merck, Serena

Moore, Roger

Razee, Charles

Schultheis, Everett

Townsend, Louis

Troutman, Warren

Waldorph, Leona Tompkins

Warner, Donald

White, Arthur

1970s

Babcock, Mary

Coggeshall, Barbara

Cunningham, Robert

Deister, Margaret

Finger, Majorie

Grant, John

Howes, Richard

Hyde, Katherine

Kreitler, Sally

Merck, Serena

Mirabile, Charles

Moore, Roger

Razzee, Charles

Renfree, Edward

Rossman, Jerome, Jr.

Rudd, John

Schultheis

Seinsheimer, Walter

Von Stade, Susan

Warner, Donald

White, Arthur

<u>1980s</u>

Adams, Lonnie

Aubin, Bruce

Babcock, Mary

Chandler, John Jr.

Cloney, Gerard

Coggeshall, Barbara

Cunningham, Robert

Farr, Olivia Hatch

Fazzone, Roger

Finger, Marjorie

Horowitz, Gerald

Hurst, Rosalie

Hyde, Katherine

Kreitler, Sally

Merck, Serena

Metzger, Mark

Mirabile, Charles

Moore, Roger

Renfree, Edward

Rossman, Jerome Jr.

Rudd, John

Segalla, John

Seinsheimer, Walter

Sollar, Arnold

Tillett, Willilam

Von Stade, Susan

Warner, Donald

1990s

Babcock, Mary

Belcher, Karen

Buckley, Priscilla

Cloney, Gerard

Coggeshall, Barbara

Dempsey, Patricia

Farr, Olivia

Fazzone, Roger

Herman, Stephan

Horowitz, Gerald

Kellogg, Kit

Lynford, Tondra Abrams

Lyons, Joan

Metzger, Mark

Rossman, Jerome Jr.

Rudd, John

Schmidt, William

Shane, William

Shinbaum, Dianne

Sollar, Arnold

Staine, Dorothy

Tillett, William

Whalen, George Jr.

Wills, Ray

Wilson, Ron

"Committee 2000"

Belcher, James

Belcher, Karen

Bollinger, Donald

Crane, Pamela

Dempsey, John

Evans, Jeanette

Evans, Whitney

Farr, Olivia

Fazzone, Roger

Lynford, Jeffrey

Santag, Howard

Shane, William

Sollar, Arnold

Sollar, Siema

2000s

Audia, Robert

Belcher, Karen

Buckley, Priscilla

Chiusano, Charles

Davis, Nancy

Dempsey, Pamela

Farr, Olivia

Fazzone, Roger

Halle, Amanda

Howes, Richard

Jacobs, Alan

Jenkins, Karen

Konkolics, Donna

Linden, Ann

Metzger, Mark

Panichi, Emil

Richards, Paul

Rossman, Jermone Jr.

Shane, William

Steinhaus, William

Whalen, George Jr.

Willis, Raymond

Wilson, Ron

2010s

Audia, Robert

Besket, Jodi

Buckley, Priscilla

Chiusano, Charles

Constantino, Jim

Cullen, Diana

Davis, Nancy

Etkin, Bruce

Fazzone, Roger

Halle, Amanda

Jacobs, Alan

Konkolics, Donna

Linden, Ann

Metzger, Mark

Mulligan, Eileen

Murphy, Don

Panichi, Emil

Richards, Paul

Rossman, Jerome Jr.

Scuccimarra, Lorraine

Steinhaus, William

Troiano, Roxanne

Whalen, George III

Whalen, George Jr.

MAPLEBROOK SCHOOL, INC.
SUMMARY OF SCHOOL INFORMATION

SCHOOL YEAR	NUMBER OF STUDENTS	ANNUAL BUDGET		NUMBER OF FULL AND PART-TIME FACULTY	ADMIN	ALL STAFF	ACRES OF LAND	NUMBER OF BUILDINGS	ADDITIONS OR RENOVATIONS
1990-91	69	$1,683,200		14	9	50	29.5	14	
		A	$24,400						
		C	$23,000						
1991-92	72	$1,866,450		14	10	50	33.72	14	Major renovation to Sky's the Limit Hall. Purchased land from Flood - 4.22 acres near Wilson Hall.
		A	$25,400						
		C	$24,700						
1992-93	75	$1,911,300		18	11	52	44.39	16	Major renovation to Wilson Hall. Purchased land and buildings known as Millpond from Twigg – 10.67 acres.
		A	$25,900						
		C	$25,500						
1993-94	82	$2,029,300		21	11	57	44.39	16	Added second floor addition to Evans Hall for staff. Renovated old barn to academic student center. Added a room on the Windridge Cottage apartment.
		A	$26,900						
		C	$26,900						

Year									
1994-95	85	$2,336,700 A $27,900 C $27,900	21	12	59	44.39	17	Built horse barn and fencing on West Campus.
1995-96	93	$2,479,600 A $28,850 C $28,850	21	12	56	44.39	18	Began construction of the new gymnasium. Renovated Windridge garage to staff house.
1996-97	97	$2,871,650 A $29,950 C $29,950	21	12	56	44.39	18	Built a new soccer field and track on lower field. Built two new tennis courts.
1997-98	104	$3,184,824 A $31,750 C $31,750	22	12	61	77.61	18	Renovated old gymnasium to theatre, library and computer center. Renovated old maintenance shop to dorm rooms. Purchased land known as the North Campus from the Dutchess Land Conservancy - 33.22 acres.

WHERE DREAMS COME TRUE

MAPLEBROOK
SCHOOL, INC.
SUMMARY OF SCHOOL INFORMATION

7/25/2017

SCHOOL YEAR	NUMBER OF STUDENTS	ANNUAL BUDGET		NUMBER OF FULL AND PART-TIME FACULTY	ALL ADMIN	STAFF	ACRES OF LAND	NUMBER OF BUILDINGS	ADDITIONS OR RENOVATIONS
1998-99	108	$3,556,330		24	14	66	77.61	21	Began construction of two duplexes on the CAPS campus one for staff and one for students. Built horse barn and fencing on North Campus. Built a new soccer field on North Campus.
		A	$32,450						
		C	$32,450						
1999-2000	109	$3,750,964		26	14	70	121.42	22	Purchased land from Linden - 40 acres. Purchased land and buildings from Bailey - 3.81 acres. Renovated old horse barn to CAPS Student Center.
		A	$34,250						
		C	$33,450						
2000-01	112	$3,942,024		24	15	80	86.1	22	Added an addition on to kitchen and dining room. Installed sprinkler system in girls dormitory. Added a second staff duplex on the CAPS Campus.

Year		A	C							
2001-02	115	A $35,350	C $34,550							Sold North Campus - 33.22 Acres. Subdivided and sold 2.1 acres near Wilson Hall.
										Began construction of Babcock Hall.
		A $37,500	C $36,650	$4,184,800	26	15	78	87	23	Purchased land and buildings from Ahearn. Relocated crosswalk on Route 22.
2002-03	115	A $38,900	C $37,950	$4,321,485	28	15	79	87	24	Competed construction on Babcock Hall
2003-04	117			$4,654,254	29	15	75	87	24	Construction of two new athletic fields.
										Installed sprinkler system in Evans Hall.
		A $39,900	C $39,450							Renovated Level II - Two classrooms
2004-05	116									Began construction of new academic building
		A $41,900	C $41,500	$4,841,717	29	15	77	97.85	29	Purchased land and buildings known as MelBrooke House - 10.01 acres.

MAPLEBROOK SCHOOL, INC.
SUMMARY OF SCHOOL INFORMATION

7/25/2017

SCHOOL YEAR	NUMBER OF STUDENTS	ANNUAL BUDGET	NUMBER OF FULL AND PART-TIME		ALL STAFF	ACRES OF LAND	NUMBER OF BUILDINGS	ADDITIONS OR RENOVATIONS
			FACULTY	ADMIN				
2005-06	115	$5,028,775 A $43,900 C $43,500	29	10 / 5	79	97.85	29	Competed construction on Thalheimer Hall
2006-07	108	$5,018,508 A $46,400 C $45,700	23	10 / 5	78	97.85	29	Completed $3.5 million capital campaign
2007-08	109	$5,410,550 A $48,700 C $47,950	23	10 / 5	79	92.25	29	Completed construction of Chapel
2008-09	111	$5,721,363	22	10 / 5	78	92.25	29	Subdivided and sold 5.6 acres from TLC property

	71.5	A	$51,200						Woodcliff Renovation
	39.5	C	$50,450						
2009-10	107		$5,618,006	21	11 / 5	78	92.25	29	
	69	A	$52,700						
	40	C	$51,950						
2010-11	88		$4,778,896	18	10 / 5	69	92.25	28	Began construction of new dining hall
	54	A	$54,700						
	34	C	$53,950						
2011-12	89		$5,399,000	19	10 / 5	67	92.25	28	Renovated Howes Hall
	55	A	$56,700						Completed construction of dining hall
	34	C	$55,950						
2012-13	97.5		$5,724,667	18	10 / 5	67	92.25	29	Began iPad program for seniors
	63.5	A	$59,000						
	34	C	$58,250						

MAPLEBROOK
SCHOOL, INC.
SUMMARY OF SCHOOL INFORMATION

7/25/2017

SCHOOL YEAR	NUMBER OF STUDENTS	ANNUAL BUDGET	NUMBER OF FULL AND PART-TIME FACULTY	ADMIN	ALL STAFF	ACRES OF LAND	NUMBER OF BUILDINGS	ADDITIONS OR RENOVATIONS
2013-14	99	$6,087,108	19	8 / 7	68	92.25	28	Created Hilfiger Hall
	61	A $59,500						Renovated Maples Apartment
	38	C $59,250						
2014-15	101.5	$6,240,255	16	9 / 9	72	92.25	28	Renovated Fazzone Hall and staff apartment
	56	A $61,500						Added porch and AC to Feig Theatre
	45.5	C $61,250						
2015-16	99	$6,635,275	16	8 / 9	77	92.25	28	Put on addition to Student Union
	57.5	A $62,500						
	41.5	C $62,250						
2016-17	102.5	$6,461,685	16	0?	76	92.25	28	Began construction on natatorium
	51	A $63,500						Began construction on Sollar Hall
	51.5	C $63,250						

Bibliography and Sources of Information

Sam Blumenthal, *Is Public Education Necessary – page 84*

Calvin Stone, *Community collaboration and the restricting of schools 1992*

Victor Bondi, *American Decades 1930-1939, pages 118 and 1995*

David Contosta, William Cutler, *Episcopal Diocese of Pennsylvania 2012*

Mary Baker Eddy, *Science and Health with Key to the scriptures, 1891*

Samara Yearbooks 1967 – 2016

Interviews/Conversations

- Betty Howes

- Rick Howes

- Dick Howes

- Jerry Rossman

- Roger Moore

- Margret Deister

- Harry Barnes

- Peter Rossman

- George Caswell

- George Whalen, Jr.

CPSIA information can be obtained
at www.ICGtesting.com
Printed in the USA
BVOW03s1035241217
503608BV00001B/44/P

9 781432 778927